PEBBLES

in the

POND

*Transforming the World
One Person at a Time*

~Wave Three~

Also By Christine Kloser

A DAILY DOSE OF LOVE
Everyday Inspiration to Help You Remember
What Your Heart Already Knows

PEBBLES IN THE POND
Transforming the World One Person at a Time
(Wave One)

PEBBLES IN THE POND
Transforming the World One Person at a Time
(Wave Two)

CONSCIOUS ENTREPRENEURS
A Radical New Approach to Purpose, Passion and Profit

THE FREEDOM FORMULA
How to Put Soul in Your Business
and Money in Your Bank

INSPIRATION TO REALIZATION
Real Women Reveal Proven Strategies for Personal,
Business, Financial and Spiritual Fulfillment

PEBBLES

in the

POND

Transforming the World
One Person at a Time

~Wave Three~

Transformation Books
York, PA

Pebbles in the Pond: Transforming the World One Person at a Time (Wave Three)

Published by:
Transformation Books
211 Pauline Drive #513
York, PA 17402
www.TransformationBooks.com

ISBN: 978-0-9851407-6-2
Library of Congress Control No: 2014939435

Cover design by Sarah Barrie
Layout and typesetting by Ranilo Cabo
Editor: Marlene Oulton, www.MarleneOulton.com
Proofreader: Gwen Hoffnagle

Printed in the United States of America

A portion of the proceeds from the sale of this book will be donated to the causes the publisher supports.

Help Me Be...

Strong enough to be vulnerable.

Wise enough to realize how little I know.

Loving enough to embrace my "enemy."

Tender enough to be powerful.

Smart enough to realize I can't do it alone.

Brilliant enough to shine the light of others.

Doubtful enough to know the power of faith.

Courageous enough to share my truth.

~Christine Kloser

Table of Contents

Introduction

THANK YOU FOR FOLLOWING THE WHISPER in your heart to pick up this book and crack open the cover. My guess is – like the contributors to this book – you've been on a powerful, transformational journey that sometimes joyously surprises you and other times throws you an unexpected curve ball that knocks you to your knees.

Perhaps as you read this you're in the middle of the most challenging time of your life. Or maybe you've just come through a difficult situation with a renewed sense of faith and hope. Perhaps you have a niggling sense that a growth opportunity is lurking around the corner waiting for you, but you just don't know what it is… yet.

No matter where you stand right now on your path, I trust that since you're here – taking time to read this book – you believe in the concept of a "pebble in the pond" and share in the vision of a world that is transformed one person at a time.

While world transformation may seem like a far-fetched dream, the truth I've come to know is that as we transform as individuals, we *do* make a difference in the lives of those around us. And if you've ever thrown a stone in a still pond, you know that one single splash sends ripples outward in every direction, creating more and more ripples. It's the same thing when that "splash" is the impact of your life and how you live it each and every day – the impact expands.

It doesn't matter if you're a leading-edge entrepreneur, schoolteacher, mom, rocket scientist, doctor, writer, healer, manager, salesperson, nurse, volunteer, retiree, or anything else; your life – and how you live it – can be a force for good in our world. Every person has the power to make a difference, including you, and that's exactly what this book is about.

At this time in history we are on the precipice of experiencing the new world many people have been dreaming about – a world filled with love, cooperation, contribution, service, community, and abundance for all. And there are a growing number of people who are doing all they can to heal themselves, become a part of the solution (simply by being who they truly and authentically are), and bring more light and love into the world.

In the pages of this book you'll meet such visionary leaders and world-changers. You might recognize some of the contributors as bestselling authors and leading entrepreneurs. Others aren't as well known, yet their stories are testaments to the power of one person's transformational journey to send ripples of good into the world.

I personally feel so blessed to receive the gift of working closely with most of the contributors to this book. We've gathered together over the course of eight months to birth this book in service to you. As you discover each contributor's story, you'll see why I consider it a blessing to call them my clients, soul travelers, and friends. *Pebbles in the Pond - Wave Three* is only possible because of the love and light they bring to the world.

Some chapters will make you cry, while others will make you laugh. Some will touch your heart deeply, while others will inspire you to think differently. Some chapters will be difficult to read as you hear of the challenges a few of the authors have faced that nobody should ever have to live through. And others will offer you a heartfelt reassurance that if they can do it (whatever the "it" is), you can, too.

So as you proceed through this book, don't feel the need to read the chapters in order. Chances are as you peruse the table of contents or randomly flip open the pages, you will receive exactly the message that is meant for you in that moment.

Above all else, let the stories in this book bathe you in love, compassion, understanding, and inspiration to transform your challenges and struggles (large or small) into beautiful blessings for yourself and others.

You never know what miracle may happen as a result of reading one of these stories. In fact, this book series in and of itself is evidence of the miraculous grace that appeared during the most challenging time of my life. In the first "wave" of *Pebbles in the Pond* (published 2012), the title of my chapter was "The Best 'Worst' Time of My Life."

It was the worst time because I was going through personal bankruptcy and a very challenging dissolution of a business partnership, unsure about how I was going to support my family and questioning everything about who I knew myself to be. Saying I felt like a failure puts it mildly. Yet that challenging time opened my heart in ways I never knew possible – and one of the many "gifts in the challenge" was the concept for this book series.

With this — Wave Three of *Pebbles in the Pond* — the ripples continue to encompass and empower you to be who you are here to be... and to let your light shine!

On behalf of myself and all of the contributing authors of this series, we send you our deepest blessings that this book delivers the inspiration and transformation your soul is seeking. May you be guided by grace.

Love and blessings,

Christine Kloser,
Spiritual Guide ~ Award Winning Author
Transformational Book Coach ~ Publisher

Frank Sinatra Was Right – Do It Your Way

Christine Kloser

IT WAS THE MORNING OF DECEMBER 1ST, 2011, and I was getting dressed to speak at an event in Baltimore, Maryland. This was my first live speaking engagement after having gone through a "dark night of the soul" in 2010.

That dark night was the most challenging thing I'd ever experienced. I had gone from having a relatively successful business, a best-selling book, being the "picture" of success, to losing it all – my home, my business (through a challenging partnership dissolution), almost my marriage… right down to having to file for bankruptcy.

Today when I look back on what had happened to get me to that dark place, I realize that I hadn't been true to myself. I had been chasing some illusion of what I thought I "should" be doing, how I thought my business "should" look, who I "should" be working with, and how I "should" be working with them.

There was a moment earlier in 2010 when I'd had to decide if I'd keep doing what I "should" do, or let it all go to discover what I was *born* to do! While it was challenging to let go of everything I was familiar with, my soul knew it was the only choice. And I was led on an amazing personal and spiritual journey that transformed my life.

Long story short, I was shown that I needed to stop trying to make money by teaching other people how to make money. That was a behavior I had slipped into, not realizing how far away it was from my true heart's desire... which was to heal hearts and transform people's lives. I had simply modelled what I saw other successful home-based entrepreneurs doing, but hadn't done the deep dive into discovering what was right and true for me.

In addition to seeing what I was *not* meant to do, it became crystal clear what I *was* meant to do. I was supposed to serve transformational authors – even though at the time I had no idea what a transformational author was. I had to define it, because on all of Google I couldn't find one reference to this thing called a "transformational author." Now it seems like such a common term... but not in 2011.

Having this insight come to me was a huge relief. Everything about it felt right. I knew authorship (since I'd been training authors for years), and I knew transformation, especially after the personal journey I'd been on, so why not combine these two passions?

While 2011 started with a tremendous amount of pain, that pain was followed by blessings and miracles too numerous to count. I defined what it meant to be a transformational author, put together a program called the Transformational Author Experience®, and got myself and my family back on our feet financially. But better than that, I experienced tremendous joy and ease serving nearly 10,000 authors in that one year.

Life was good.

So back to that morning on December 1st, 2011, and that speaking engagement. It was not just a "coming out" after my dark night of the soul... it was a day that would transform my life.

Transformation comes in so many forms. Some of it occurs by a proverbial two-by-four to the head (bankruptcy was one of my two-by-fours), other times it comes in a whisper, a loving face, or a quiet moment of reflection.

This day, transformation occurred in my closet! (It really can happen anywhere at any time.)

There I was, digging through my closet to find my fancy speaking suit... the one that had been packed away for the past year. It was a beautiful brown tailored suit with a long coat and pants that fit like they were custom made for me. I had a sparkly top to wear underneath and the perfect pair of shoes to complement the outfit.

I got myself dressed in that suit as I'd done before and looked in the mirror. But this time I didn't like what I saw at all. In fact, I cringed and wanted to jump out of my skin! Or that suit to be exact!

Who *was* that person in the mirror wearing that fancy suit? That suit used to feel like a second skin to me and now I wanted to get out of it as fast as I could. Why was that happening?

When I looked in the mirror, what I saw was someone who put on a costume to try to look a certain way – together, successful, sharp, smart, etc. I instantly recalled one other time in particular when I wore that suit and felt like I needed it to hold me together, because if people knew what was really inside me and the struggles I faced, they wouldn't listen to a word I said. It felt like if people knew the real me, they would be anything but impressed, which was important to me. I had always strived to be good enough and liked by other people.

I used to be so comfortable with the "dress for success/dress to impress" model. Anytime I'd travel to speak or attend an event, I would spend days thinking about what I'd wear. Would I fit in? What should I wear to give off a certain air of confidence? (Mind you, confidence I didn't have on the inside!) My patient husband would sit through hours of my trying on outfits, giving me his opinions until I found just the right thing that would show others I was successful.

If I faked it – success – enough, then eventually I'd make it, right? Not so true. If you fake it too long, you miss the gift of discovering the true you.

So as I looked at myself in the mirror that morning, my path became clear. Finally I didn't have to fake it anymore. Finally I knew in the depth of my being that I didn't need a suit to impress anyone. Finally I knew who I was, and it didn't matter if I wore a fancy suit, yoga pants, jeans, or a dress. Clothes don't make me who I am... I am who I am because of the inside of me!

Some of the stories you'll read in this book share far more challenging experiences than mine, and moments of transformation that are profound. But that morning when I looked in the mirror was one of the most transformational moments of my life. And I'm sharing it with you so you can look for the seemingly small moments in your life that can hold the gift of your next transformation.

Okay... on with the story!

As the clock ticked away and I needed to leave for the speaking engagement, I tore through my closet trying to find something that looked and felt RIGHT! I put on all of my old speaking outfits – the tailored pants, fancy shoes, and sparkly tops – NONE of them felt like me! They all felt like I was putting them on just for show.

The only thing in my closet that felt right was my favorite pair of jeans and one of my long cardigan sweaters. But I thought, "I can't wear jeans for a speaking engagement... that's so unprofessional. What will people think?!"

I'm sure that my inner critic was alive and well from my days of being told I couldn't wear jeans to church... that I needed to look nice. I had always interpreted that to mean I should look nice for other people, because they (or God) would judge me based on what I wore. That may not be true, but that's what it felt like to me as a kid.

Then, standing in my closet, I heard the words of Frank Sinatra rolling around in my head singing, "I did it my way." Guess what: so did I!

I put on my jeans, a simple tank top, and my favorite cardigan sweater. The only thing that I kept from my fancy outfit was the great pair of shoes. I felt amazing! I felt like me! I felt like I could walk on that stage and be 100 percent authentically me.

This might seem like a small thing, but it was truly liberating for me! I hadn't realized how much time and energy I'd spent worrying about what others would think of me based on what I wore – time and energy that would have been much better spent serving and helping others on their transformational journeys.

So this is what I do now. I enjoy my time doing work I love… with people I love to do it with. While I like to get "dressed" now and then, I haven't set foot on a speaking stage in anything but jeans since that day in December of 2011. Actually I had to wear dress pants once because of a strict dress code at the venue I was speaking at, but other than that, it's jeans and a sweater for me.

And guess what? Nobody has ever said anything about my wearing jeans on stage other than how much they liked my outfit, and also how refreshing it was to see someone look like a regular person on the stage.

It's now become part of my brand, what people have come to expect from me – that I'm going to show up looking exactly like me… an authentic, down-to-earth, real, caring person who isn't putting on a show for anyone, whose presence is what people need the most.

The confidence I've gained since that morning spent digging for a suitable outfit in my closet has changed my life. While it may have just been a decision to wear jeans, it was really a decision to lay down my façade once and for all and let people see the real me.

That one decision has helped me create a successful and profitable debt-free business, help tens of thousands of authors around the world, and transform lives. In short, exactly what I was born to do.

Frank Sinatra had it right, and I'll cherish those lyrics forever: "I did it my way."

When I reflect on this book and the goal to transform the world one person at a time, I believe that when I chose to wear jeans on stage it was that one small decision that's helped me impact so many people. I do believe we are making a difference in the world. As the publisher of this book, this is just one example of that difference.

So I want to ask you now, what small thing are you doing that's compromising who you are? Do you dress a certain way, but not really feel at home in your clothes? Do you say or do things you don't really want to do just because you think you should, or wonder what others will say about you?

I encourage you to look for those small and seemingly insignificant ways you might be compromising the essence of who you are. Then heed Frank Sinatra's advice and be willing to Do It Your Way! You'll feel better and become a more open vessel for your gifts to shine through without anything getting in your way!

You deserve to do things your way – your book, speaking engagements, career, dressing, and living; you're the only one on the planet who can authentically "do" you!

Now if you'll excuse me, I need to go put on a pair of jeans and join my family for dinner.

Christine Kloser, "The Transformation Catalyst," is a spiritual guide, award winning author, and transformational book coach whose spot-on guidance transforms the lives of visionary entrepreneurs and authors around the world. Her coaching and training programs have impacted more than 50,000 authors to help them unleash their authentic voice and share their message on the pages of a book. If you have a book inside of you and want help getting it out, get started with Christine's FREE video training here: www.GetYourBookDone.com.

Developing
Your Authentic Voice

Lisa Nichols

IN SCHOOL I LEARNED VERY EARLY that I was supposed to motivate people. I was a cheerleader – I knew it. In twelfth grade I became a Commissioner of Spirit, which was someone who rallied the cheerleaders and held them all accountable for being joyful and having school spirit. Now discovering my authentic voice is another story.

Being able to speak and use words does not mean you're celebrating your authentic voice. Many of my students who work in corporate America or in organizations delivering messages come to me wanting to deliver *their* messages. They want to move from using their voices to using their *authentic* voices… and there's a difference.

It was about seventeen years ago that I began to discover the power of transparency and authenticity – the freedom of being emotionally naked when necessary. In my journey to becoming a *Chicken Soup for the Soul* author, I wrote stories for Jack Canfield to look at, and as I wrote one of them I felt a "withhold" in me, like, "Oh, I don't want to tell him that. That's a little too transparent."

But I literally couldn't write the next line; it didn't feel right to withhold like that. I had to write the truth to get to the rest of the story. In having the courage to be transparent, I began to learn that there is freedom in transparency. My grandmother says, "When you're authentic and transparent, there's nothing to hide, nothing to defend, nothing to prove, nothing to outrun, because all of a sudden you're living inside your truth."

In 2005, when Rhonda Byrne invited me to become a part of the movie *The Secret,* I didn't fully understand everything about the Law of Attraction. I grew up in a Baptist church and we didn't study that law. I embraced it, but I just wasn't aware of it. When I did the interview for *The Secret*, I simply spoke my truth, and lo and behold it was a great fit for the movie, and I became one of the featured teachers. Over and over again I kept experiencing that every time I was authentic, greater things happened than when I was shut down or when I tried to protect my inner self. See, when I tried to protect something – my image, my brand, my reputation, the fact that I was called "expert" – I withheld a piece of my authentic self, my authentic message. Energy didn't flow the way it did when I was authentic and transparent, so I continued to uncover and share all of who I am.

You can set yourself free by just being your authentic self. You liberate yourself. And better yet, you liberate those around you. The beauty of finding your authentic voice, then sharing it, is a deliberate action that starts with you, but becomes contagious. You set a pathway; you put energy out into the universe that permeates and impacts other people. It might catch someone in their darkest hour and help lift them to their own light, their own divinity. So your authenticity is actually less about you than it is about serving the planet.

When I'm authentic, I'm serving the planet. And we're all servers. If you can read my words, you are someone who is here to serve and make a difference. You might be asking yourself, "How can I leave my fingerprint on this world?" Simple: use and exercise your authentic voice and live transparently. When you simply be who you are, you embody the truth that you are enough, you are important, you matter, and you are perfectly created.

Like any other person, I have my fears. I remember in 1994 when I first said, "I want to be a speaker," and as the excitement leapt into my heart, fear jumped into my head. One was chasing the other. I remember my first fear for the first five years was who would want to listen to me? I'm an African-American woman from South Central Los Angeles. What can I contribute to the planet? The second fear was who would want to be inspired by me? I come from very simple means. You have to come from wealth to inspire people. And then the third fear was who would listen to me while I was still struggling with my weight? These fears were very real! I couldn't change my background; I'm always going to be an African-American woman; and I've dealt with my weight forever.

Instead of trying to outrun or ignore the fears, I had to turn around and confront them. When faced with such fear, I say, "Okay, wait a minute. Let me unpack it." I then write down my fears. The best way to unpack your fears is to keep diving into them by asking another question. I learned this from my wonderful brother in the work, Reverend Michael Beckwith. He said, "Keep questioning your fear until it dissipates into the nothingness that it is." So when I heard, "People won't listen to me because I'm an African-American woman," I asked myself, "How do I know?" and the answer was, "I don't know." Then I asked myself, "What if they don't listen to me?" The answer was, "Well, there are some who will." The next question was, "What if there are some who will, then what?" The answer was, "I'll speak to them." You can unpack your fears by asking the right questions.

I do this little game with myself in which I just keep asking questions to uncover the worst-case scenario. Let's say you're afraid to fall, so you never take a leap. If you never take a leap, you never can soar. Literally, you're preventing yourself from soaring because you're afraid of falling. Ask yourself, "So what if I fall?" "Oh, my leg will get hurt." "Okay, what if your leg gets hurt?" "Then I'll suffer for a while." "After you've finished suffering, what will you do?" "I'll get back up." "When you get back up, what will you do?" "Oh! Readily begin again!" The worst-case scenario is you're going to get up at some point and begin again. For the record, if I'd waited until I was my perfect ideal weight to speak, nobody would ever have heard my voice... period! Every single thing you could be afraid of you can question until it dissipates into the nothingness that it always has been and always will be.

In order to fully release that authentic voice and not let your fears stop you, I believe the first person you need to fall madly in love with is yourself. Not just like or even love yourself, but *fall madly in love with* the person you are. Not in a braggadocian way, a self-indulgent way, or one that shrinks people around you so you can feel grand, but in a way of ultimate gratitude, humility, graciousness, and honoring your brilliance. When you fall madly in love with yourself, you can be authentic to the world and say, "It's my job to give you the true me, and it's your job to do whatever you choose." When you get that, let me tell you, you've cracked the code. When you can say, "It's my job to fall madly in love with myself and give you my most authentic being, and then it's your job to do whatever it is you choose," you gain total freedom!

Another way to develop your authentic voice is to ask yourself what pain you are the solution to. What pain are you the healing balm for? Another question to ask is what joy does your message bring to the world? Either there's a joy that you bring or there's a pain that you relieve. Many people do only one or the other. For example, if you are a travel agent, you're just bringing the joy; you're not necessarily directly relieving a pain. Though people can be over-stressed and need a vacation, vacations are really scheduled from joy. You have to know what pain and what problem you are solving, or what joy you are bringing to others.

You might want to ask yourself, "How is the world a better place because my message exists?" Your answer should be very detailed. It's too broad to say, "Because people are happier." When I consider my Speak and Write live training event for aspiring authors and speakers, I say, "The world is a better place because Speak and Write exists; because people are able to come to a community and put the infrastructure around their speaking and writing business so they can create a lifestyle with it. They can create a lifetime legacy. Speak and Write helps people stop being stuck." That's the pain I release. "It also helps them find their storytelling ability." That's the joy it brings. When you want to develop your authentic voice, think about what joy you can bring, what pain you can relieve, and how the world can be a better place because you exist.

Here's the next question, and it's intense: If you don't speak and don't share your authentic voice, how will the world suffer? I know that's a heavy question to ask, but what convinces you to share your message, your authentic voice, is understanding the prize and the cost that the world will pay, or you will pay, if you don't share it. It gets to the core of you. So answer those questions: What pain, what problem are you the solution to? What joy do you bring; how is the world a better place because your message is shared with the world? And what's the cost that the world will pay if you don't?

To experience living and speaking from a place of authenticity, ask yourself, "What areas in my life do I need to pay attention to, and how do I move those particular areas of my life from where they are to where I want them to be?" Your life is big. Break it down into smaller chunks – your spiritual life; your relationships; your business endeavors; your financial life; and your physical life, meaning the physical environment of your home, the condition of your car, the condition of your office, etc. Ask yourself, "Is this where I want it to be?" Examine your connection with nature, your body, yourself – every one of those areas. When you start giving yourself what you need in each one of those areas, you'll start believing in who you are. You'll start valuing yourself more. And then you'll begin to serve people from your overflow rather than from an "empty tank."

If you're not valuing yourself and your authentic self, there's a lack of something – self-attention, self-love, spirituality, fully living in your relationships, or being in financial integrity. Whenever there's a lack in any part of your life, you'll likely begin to question your value. But don't focus solely on your value. Look at all those other areas and handle them. Give yourself what you need in each area to remove the sense of lack, and your value will naturally take care of itself.

Until I was willing to confront all areas of my life, I wasn't truly sharing my authentic voice. I had to reflect on every aspect – love, work, career, goals, and relationships. I looked at every single area and asked myself, "From where I am right now to where I want to be, what's the distance, and how do I close the gap?" When I began to value each and every area of my life, people began to follow suit, and the same thing will happen for you.

I'd like to leave you with this last thought about the beauty of developing your authentic voice. Remember that every decision you've ever made was based on what you knew at the time. No mistake lasts forever. And it's in your imperfection that you're perfect for your Divine assignment. When you say yes to something – that bold "YES" with knees knocking and teeth chattering, saying yes to your greatness, grandness, and brilliance – you allow the God in you to be used and to come through you, and the world becomes a better place. You can get knocked down. That's okay, because once you've found your authentic voice you're always prepared to get back up. You can run and you can leap, because you've been designed to soar. That's who you are. You might not soar initially; you might crawl, then walk, then run... ah, but then you soar. And believe me, soaring is your birthright.

Lisa Nichols is a bestselling author, a popular public speaker, a powerful coach, and a charismatic teacher. She's reached millions in America and internationally with her powerful message of service, excellence, empowerment, and gratitude. Her participation in the self-development phenomenon, *The Secret,* catapulted her popularity across the globe. She's now appeared on the *Oprah Winfrey Show*, *Extra*, *Larry King Live*, and NBC's Emmy Award-winning show, *Starting Over*. Learn more at www.MotivatingTheMasses.com.

A Night at the Movies Can Make a Difference

Andrea Rockstein-Ahrens

The Awakening

I WAS THIRTY-SEVEN YEARS OLD and considered myself a happy person when a movie titled *The Experiment* hit the German movie theatres. The movie starts out in a pleasant manner: In anticipation of earning extra money, volunteers apply to participate in the experiment without knowing what is about to happen to them. Some are assigned to be prisoners who have to follow rules and some are assigned to be wardens who ensure the rules are obeyed without having to use their batons. At first the atmosphere in prison is relaxed. But the situation quickly gets out of control and the wardens increasingly resort to violent measures to ensure order. One inmate is about to be forced to drink a full liter of milk even though he is allergic to milk. A second prisoner who rushes to his aid and drinks the milk for him is punished. This heroic deed doesn't save the inmate with the allergy from his fate for long, as he dies as a result of continued ill-treatment by the wardens.

While watching the movie I suffered right along with the inmates. Suddenly I felt a knife-stabbing pain in my gut. I felt tension in my body. Right there and then I became aware of how tense I was and how familiar that feeling was to me – how common tension was a part of my daily life. A scene that a director had used to stage a psychological thriller set off a cascade of questions within me that needed answers. What was the reason for this tension in my everyday life? Was my everyday life perhaps not quite as nice as I wanted to believe? For the first time I had serious doubts. After the movie I wasn't able to go home straight away. I absolutely had to sit and talk with my best friend, and we talked for hours.

How could I consider myself a happy person when I hadn't even been aware that I was suppressing a vital part of myself and of my feelings – the same kind of feelings the director used to stage a psycho-thriller like *The Experiment*? Was I normal? Could I trust myself? Who, in fact, was I?

My previous behavioral patterns and beliefs had helped me finish school and get through my apprenticeship as an industrial clerk. I'd worked my way up to the office of the chairman of the board of Volkswagen. These patterns had helped me successfully study economics, build a career, and get to know a man who had sat next to me at the cinema, and for whom I felt so much that I decided to stay in Germany instead of accepting an offer to go to Italy. But reflecting on my decisions, I asked myself, "Where does this tension come from? Can I trust my feelings?"

The First Cautious Steps Towards a New Direction

I slowly began to reflect on who I was and what I wanted to achieve for myself and my life, and why. It took a while, but I received answers. And within three years I had been promoted to director. Actually I was the head of finance at one of VW's engine-manufacturing plants for automotive engines. I had gotten married, and become a mother.

What helped me do it? What had changed?

After the initial shock, I questioned the credos I had adopted in my life. One of them was "If I only work hard enough, if I try my best to fit in, I will be rewarded." But was this really true? *The Experiment* was probably much closer to reality than my set of beliefs allowed me to acknowledge, because good behavior was not necessarily rewarded. Yet I had heard more often than not that there are no such things as guarantees and justice in life.

My view of the world wasn't merely shattered by my deep thinking; it collapsed in on itself. My truth existed no longer. I felt robbed, petrified, and helpless. But as the dust began to settle, I realized that if these alleged guarantees in life did not exist, it was time to try something new. Hope burgeoned in me. Could this tension and vibration, this helplessness, seed something new and positive?

As if through an act of liberation I had permission to think the impossible: What if I did not have to force myself that hard to fit in? What if I chose not to work quite as hard since there weren't any guarantees anyway? Suddenly I could get out of the rat race and allow myself to have completely new thoughts.

Even as a child I was impressed by my parents' vigor and success. My mother was the heart of our family life and a great connector; my father always beamed with enthusiasm and love of life. His family and his profession were his existence. When I worked for the CEO of Volkswagen, I was fascinated again by the enthusiasm, decisiveness, and sometimes the ingenuity and confident manner of the executives. What if I allowed myself to think of myself as a creative person, even one who inspired people? Secretly that was one of the reasons I had studied business; I wanted to know about the serious side of life, and I wanted to make a difference while at the same time reaching out to people. But when I started my studies, only one woman had managed to make it to the top and hold a leading position at the headquarters of the Volkswagen company – one out of thousands of employees. What a revelation this new concept was to me.

Could a Genius Zone Exist for Me?

On the other hand, during my studies I had clearly decided to focus on finance issues in business. This is a field that is based on facts and figures, and provides an overview of a company. Yes, that was "my thing." Even after graduation I was fortunate to be working for great and interesting people, and was able to learn a lot from them. So what would happen if I just started "thinking bigger?" If my preconceived guarantees didn't exist, then I had nothing to lose by instituting change in my life.

In retrospect it seems almost like a little miracle. As soon as I was ready to embark on the adventure, I received an opportunity in my career that turned out to be my most interesting assignment at VW; I was appointed financial director at the manufacturing plant. This wasn't just a cherished daydream, but a dream job for real.

My Personal Proof

As soon as I got there, the first difficulties showed up. The Volkswagen Group had to cut spending, and therefore each facility had to contribute its share to the new budget. I was left with two options: use this difficulty as an excuse to bury my head in the sand and give up before even starting, or put my skills to the test. I opted for the latter. I was actually able to turn a situation that was most likely to result in an insurmountable problem into a great opportunity to grab the attention of my new colleagues, my staff, and everyone else involved. And I aimed for the obvious. I knew what they all really wanted most was to keep as much of their budget as possible.

It wasn't an easy task, but over time we agreed on compromises. Supported by a great team, the goal was within reach when the next hurdle came out of the blue. A strike brought our production line to a halt as parts deliveries stalled. Definitely an unfavorable situation to be in: no production, no output, no income to cover the ongoing fixed costs such as rent, insurance, administrative costs, and so on. How can you save money under such circumstances? In finance, creative thinking is key to finding solutions in dire situations. All employees received training on financial basics, and though their enthusiasm was limited, quickly enough it became clear to everyone how important it would be to work together. The small savings each individual group was able to achieve added up to a large sum. Not only did we reach our cost-cutting goals, we did it together. This collective experience not only made for a great team, but gave us all a sense of family and responsibility for one another.

This experience has shaped my thought processes to this day, because I had my own personal proof that it was possible to achieve economic goals and to be human at the same time. Almost ten years later, I am still invited to the annual Christmas party organized by my former staff. Although I cannot manage to be there every year, I am touched from the bottom of my heart every time I receive an invitation.

Follow Your Heart and Your Genius

In the truest sense, a seemingly simple movie can make a difference. I managed to give up my old thinking patterns and find enough courage to try new things. If that type of thinking worked once in my workplace, it would certainly work again. I would even have had the opportunity to move up the career ladder one step further if I'd stayed at that job, but a totally new challenge was waiting for me.

The man who had sat next to me at the cinema a few years before had believed in me all this time. His creed to this day is "If it makes you happy, go for it!" We decided it was time to get married and start a family. Originally I had planned to get back to work quickly after the birth of our child, and I did return when our daughter was six months old. It was wonderful. I felt reintegrated immediately, and thoroughly enjoyed my work. But our daughter didn't feel comfortable at the childcare center. My husband and I lived about three hundred kilometers apart at the time, so we only saw each other on weekends, and I was forty years old.

Again I asked myself if I was I brave enough to try new things without any guarantees. My heart answered quite loudly with something like this: "Now that you have become a mother at your age, enjoy it to the fullest."

In fact, I left Volkswagen and the group in which I had repeatedly met great people. After working there for many years I was grateful that they had given me the opportunity to develop and grow.

It almost seems like there has been a recurring pattern in my life; that after a particularly beautiful moment, another challenge is waiting for me. When I am able to handle the challenge with all of my heart, repeatedly something good occurs. After high school I had initially started my apprenticeship at VW with a heavy heart. Nonetheless I made it to the office of the chairman of the board. When I found the courage to begin my studies, I also had the strength to carry on until the end, and was rewarded with my dream job after many wonderful tasks. At the same time I attended coaching courses, originally to find out more about myself, and later to be a good boss.

When I became a mother, I felt fortunate to have a certain amount of life experience and self-confidence under my belt. Therefore the decision in favor of motherhood and a career as a self-employed coach instead of continuing in the corporate world came easily to me. I very much enjoy the love and warmth my daughter and I give each other. It is so enriching to discover the world through someone else's eyes and to see its greatness. With the same intention I accompany others on their life-journeys through my coaching.

Your Playing Small Doesn't Serve the World

"… and as we let our own light shine, we unconsciously give other people the permission to do the same." This is part of a quotation by

Marianne Williamson that I very much appreciate, as it summarizes my drive to look for the better and encourage others to do the same.

My old dogma pops up every now and then as if to test me to see if I am really interested in working hard only to end up with a small result or no result at all. I have to admit I am not fully cured of my old beliefs, but today I have come to terms with my old patterns. They have become friendly guides that remind me what to do when I find myself facing an imaginary (inner) wall, which still happens from time to time. Then I stop and ask myself why I should invest even more of my energy in the wrong place. The results won't get any better if I do!

I believe that I need as much energy to suppress a displeasing feeling (or the inner voice) as I need to start something new. I am pleased when I discover I have once more fallen victim to my old pattern and this experience will get me one step closer to my own happiness. When this happens I know it's time to find some things I can be grateful for. The next step is to pay attention to what really excites me, what touches my heart. Of course I am a human being with faults, but at the same time I try again and again to live up to my values. This is how I get the energy I need and the sense of responsibility and personal freedom that allow my mind to soar high in the sky, feeling safe even so.

Today I know I can rely on both my creativity and persistence. I have my heart in the right place and I can trust my feelings. These attributes allow me to remain curious and full of courage. And whenever I grow personally, pretty soon my income grows, too. To me money is an expression of how much I allow myself to live in harmony. Recently I learned how much energy and support you can receive from networking and exchanging ideas with like-minded people, and from femininity itself. Without these encounters this chapter would not have been written as it is today.

I am convinced that in business and politics, even when major decisions are made, the cooperation of people is of much greater influence today. That is why it is so important to be vigilant about how we treat each other and to support one another. We all have our own history, our good and bad sides, experiences, talents, abilities, and difficulties. Putting these different pieces of the puzzle together so that clarity, trust, and inner peace can occur is what counts; combined with gratitude and enthusiasm, great things are possible. Each of us is brilliant, talented, and unique. Everyone has their own genius. As we change and grow beyond limits to achieve true greatness, our actions provide the freedom for others to do the same.

Discover-your-Genius Expert **Andrea Rockstein-Ahrens** empowers creative female leaders to discover their genius in as few as 90 days and capitalize on it to skyrocket their incomes. A keynote speaker on "Women's Wealth," Andrea's genius comes alive guiding audiences, clients, and event participants to live their lives and businesses in line with their true callings. She supports charismatic women in welcoming prosperous new lives as profitable and feminine entrepreneurs. Andrea's own life is proof positive of her methods. Learn more at www.Get-Paid-for-Your-Genius.com.

Lead a Perspective Revolution: Your Biggest Obstacles Can Become Your Greatest Opportunities

Candace Asher

It's All Part of the Plan

"Truth only reveals itself when one gives up all preconceived ideas."
~ Shoseki

"IT'S ALL PART OF THE PLAN," said a voice that was not my own. I'd just watched my foster parents beat their dog, Rinny, silly. This was my third foster home since age two; I was now three. Rinny had scarfed down steaks they'd left defrosting on the counter.

"Why didn't they put them on top of the refrigerator where a dog couldn't reach them?" I wondered.

"Because they're ignorant," said the voice inside.

Since I would be their next victim, it was helpful to receive the voice's guidance for the first time in my young life. I learned that my foster parents' aggression was not my fault. I would come to realize that hurtful behavior fielded against me had *nothing* to do with me and *everything* to do with the wars raging inside of others. Just as important, I sensed I'd attracted these experiences from a "Source lesson plan."

"Go pee," my foster father would say. That was code for "you're getting beaten." Dad didn't want me to urinate on him from my uncontrollable trembling, so he entered the bathroom as soon as I flushed. He'd take off his belt, sit on the edge of the bathtub, and flip me onto his lap. I suffered welts on my butt for days. Later that day he'd take me to the soda shop for an ice pop. Decades afterward I figured out why I consistently had passive-aggressive relationships in life. Thanks to the work I've done – and the Source lesson plan – I've left that pattern behind.

Those foster parents were unhappy people, struggling through unfulfilled lives. But like any good opponent, they played a strong role in helping me remain true to my best self. The internal discomfort they created for me tipped me off about where I might've gotten confusedly stuck by human evil. My education about new boundaries being the gifts I can give myself my entire lifetime had begun. Deliverance continues to be the plan (so long as I keep polishing my discernment lens!).

I thought the guidance and foundational principles I received growing up were ordinary. Now I know that's not so. I was lucky that I believed my challenges were leading me to stand in the light of self-value. I've come to believe I was given the capacity for deep insight so that I would not only become victorious over victimizing energies in my own life, but also help others do the same. I've come to call this leading a "perspective revolution."

The Soul's Healing Journey

My fascination with my soul's journey took on the form of a jigsaw puzzle. Its pieces included whom my soul would connect and disconnect with, be parented or abandoned by, and get seduced, loved, or abused by.

Relationship by relationship, I sense my soul's healing journey at play. I work not to get stuck with any one viewpoint. I strive to figure out how the pieces fit together. I also aim to be a curse-breaker.

What does that mean? For example, at age fifteen I stood up to abuse in a foster home and demanded my walking papers. I preferred to go to an orphanage. Then *that same day*, I was miraculously rescued by a friend's mom who asked me to become part of their family.

Another time I was saved from a house fire thanks to being at a sleepover I persisted in asking to go to after years of being refused permission to do so. The night of the sleepover, the heater in the cellar of my foster home blew up. *It burned down the entire house.* If I'd been there I would have died. Instead I safely slept at the home of my friend, who, ironically, was the daughter of the chief of the fire department. Hmm, part of the plan?

All of this has given me an ongoing capacity to view and experience life as if I were watching a movie filmed out of sequence. I appreciate the many angles and changing hues. Obstacles are dominant in one frame, and opportunities in another. Eventually they bleed into each other. Unresolved issues in one relationship show up in another until I figure out the lesson I'm supposed to learn. The lesson? Without living through and understanding darkness, I can't recognize or return to the light.

By partially or completely changing my perspective, I can change my life. I am fortunate in this because I have been steamrolled in my journey. I'm now able to trust that while being snuffed out on some levels, there is also *emergent light* shining and pulling me forward. Death of certain aspects of my life leads me to be reborn in others – one clan, one relationship, one experience at a time.

What's the overriding bottom line? To hold to the *emergent light*. To keep my focus on burning off the opponents' annihilation efforts so I can remain in the light. It's my ongoing perspective revolution.

Your Perspective Revolution and Raising the Bar

"You must do the thing you think you cannot do."

~ Eleanor Roosevelt

I wholeheartedly agree with Eleanor Roosevelt. For me that means striving to make challenges work *for* me, not *against* me. I call this raising the bar. This means surpassing previous accomplishments in both my personal and professional endeavors while accepting and embracing my resistance with compassion and hard work. I look for where my setbacks can serve me as growth opportunities. That's how I begin raising the bar. Then I ask, "What thoughts, feelings, and behaviors can I choose to take charge of?" And each time I take a proactive step, I find I can both wash away negativity and build up resilience.

Every revolution is about an overthrow of something. Perhaps your current perspective about your own challenges must be overthrown. Based on experience, I encourage you to figure out how your challenges might work *for* you. It really is our problems that tweak us back into shape. How do you do this? By paying attention to the way problems tap you on the shoulder or kick you in the butt. They can wake you up and help you begin again. So look forward. *Look toward the emergent light!*

To facilitate your perspective revolution, I have written a song about *making your challenges work for you and not against you*. It is called "SOAPSQUARED™" (SOAP²™), and it's also the theme song for my new training program, SOAPSQUARED – RAISE THE BAR™. In this program, the SOAPSQUARED – RAISE THE BAR™ formula teaches you how to lead your own perspective revolution and bring out the best in yourself.

The first time I *raised the bar*, it was actually a literal experience! I was living on an isolated back road with my cruelest foster family. I was already nine and I'd never had a bicycle. I was out in the barn-like garage where I discovered a rusty, old, cobweb-covered Schwinn bike

30

in a gigantic junk pile. I tore out of the garage and ran to my foster parents. "Can I have the bike that I found in the garage?" They told me I could. Then I asked, "Would either of you teach me how to ride it?" Do you know they both refused? You can't imagine how much that bicycle meant to me: freedom, fun, friendships down the road, and the chance to seize back a measure of control in a life that had already gone waaay out of control. To this day this story serves me as I face new challenges.

Do you remember how hard it was to learn to ride a bike, even when you had help? I was heartbroken to go it alone, but right before my eyes that rusty old bicycle seemed to turn into a golden chariot treasure, calling to me, "Come! You don't need help from anybody else! Come! I can show you a great big world of possibilities out there! Come! Let me show you the way!"

So instead of having a temper tantrum or a pity party, I reached past the cobwebs and splintered boards, and *I raised the bar of that kickstand!* Then I wheeled that chariot out of the swelteringly hot garage into the cool morning air. I worked hard to reach my tippy toes all the way down to the pedals of that giant contraption while aiming to keep the handlebars facing forward. I wiped out again and again, but I kept at it. I swatted away mosquitos and bees, kissed my scraped palms and bruised knees, and each time I wiped out, I got back up and began again.

Hours later the moment finally came when suddenly I could rest my feet on the tops of the pedals, keep my balance, and hold the handlebars facing forward without falling over! Absolutely *thrilling* and *empowering*. Fun, joy, power and pride, the likes of which I'd never known! By sundown I could ride the whole way down Majestic Road and play with kids in the neighborhood who had a swimming pool!

This bicycle challenge taught me that by raising the bar, my *biggest* obstacle could indeed become my *greatest* opportunity.

By participating in my obstacle and raising the bar when I've recently faced much more difficult challenges (like a flood recovery, selling a home, and building a business), I continue to rely on that profound childhood lesson. It never crossed my mind that I would not achieve my goal that day. Since that day it's been instilled in me that *on my own* I can reach for and fulfill my dreams – which I've done. For example, I've written and recorded original songs and toured seven countries in Europe with a record that had five Top 10 hits. That was my big break into the music business – all while on the far side of forty!

Then, right at the half-century mark of my life, divorce came and I took some brutal falls. But as with that bike, the scrapes and bruises have served me to raise the bar again and again. In recent times I've often had to find balance on my own because there has been nobody to keep me from falling. Sometimes it involves my hitting the ground and getting back up. Today I've risen back up – as a speaker, entrepreneur, and author.

Leading a Perspective Revolution

"Much of life is about maintaining possibility behavior
in the face of seemingly impossible circumstances."
~ Max W. Dixon

The same voice that tipped me off in the past about other people's inner wars spoke to me again one day while I was sitting by a creek talking to God. I asked, "Why am I so afraid of transferring colleges and moving to a new apartment? It feels so foreign to be this afraid." I waited. I listened. And I heard, "You will be raped." Oh! So that's what my fierce anxiety was about. Oh my God!

Several weeks later I volunteered to be the roommate who stayed at home for the plumber to come and fix our bathroom tub. What I got instead was a knife held at my throat by an imposter plumber who raped me. To cope, I relied on my understanding of another's inner wars (as I'd first learned from my foster parents).

I don't know if one ever completely heals from rape. The streets are never quite the same. However, decades later, one of the soul-clearing aspects of my healing seems related to my having been a fetus in my mother's womb while she was incestuously raped by her father, my grandfather.

Raising the bar and returning to a clean slate is no light affair. I believe that sometimes life gives us repeated *content* traumas that can help us return to our original purity of *form*, similar to when a shaman gives a snakebite victim survivable snakebite poison to counteract the venom.

In this vast universe of interdependent events, that kind of perception and perspective revolution is what I bring to my challenges to reclaim my best, pure self. I work at building my capacity *to cancel out negative imprints and wash them away.* Our predispositions and inherited propensities become our unique assignments from which to disentangle and heal. Reaching beyond the obvious, I dig deep into my challenges to find what lies hidden.

No matter what challenges you face, you can always view them through a different lens. That's your perspective revolution waiting — one that can lead you back to a clean slate and put you in touch with your basic goodness.

Finding the Best of Yourself

"If we can bring ourselves down by our karma, surely it is
in our power to raise ourselves by it."
~ Swami Vivekananda

I believe God is singing a big song through the stories of all of our lives. Oddly, my first work as a presenter was at fundraising events, singing songs on behalf of sexual abuse centers. Perhaps the lyrics of my SOAPSQUARED™ song — born of my many triumphs — will inspire you!

When the selfish, greedy, jealous ones try to cut you
down to size, raise the bar!
Denying cowards, lying bullies teach us to hold our heads
up high, raise the bar!
Don't let the tears you cry do nothing but put
courage in your hearts.
Don't be afraid, be brave, stand tall, SOAP UP,
Raise the Bar!

I've found that the most disappointing and heartbreaking tragedies can fill me with hope and meaning in a world I don't always understand. I think that our intentions and mindsets play a great hand in turning our circumstances to our favor. What has been imprinted into the depths of my challenges is, ironically, also what lifts me up.

I urge you to be patient and compassionate with yourself. Some perspective revolutions can take an entire lifetime to accomplish.

How might the most awful thing you've experienced help you transform your life and find your way forward? Do you dare reach for all the possibilities? Might your challenges help you find out just how magnificent you are?

Embrace Your Resistance with Compassion

"Toleration is the greatest gift of mind; it requires the same effort of the brain that it takes to balance oneself on a bicycle."
~ Helen Keller

Are you ready to embrace your resistance with compassion and entertain that your challenges might offer more than problems? Chances are they are your growth opportunities lurking!

Chances are, too, that the seeds for an actual revolution have been planted within your obstacle itself. What kind of revolution? *A perspective revolution*. That means recognizing that the life experiences that drive you crazy are likely to become the seeds of your transformation. Your capacity to penetrate *and* tolerate such paradoxes is the key to becoming everything you'd like to be. Let challenges serve you as springboards to the successful life you're meant to live!

With the eyes of my expanded heart I've come to see what my naked eye cannot. In that way my holy adventure continues to make a modicum of human sense. I figure it's all part of the Source lesson plan!

Candace Asher, founder of Relentless Resilience, is a corporate trainer, an internationally acclaimed recording artist/songwriter, and an "in the trenches" Resilience Expert. Having beaten tremendous odds surviving abusive foster homes, rape, a flood, being on welfare, divorce, and unemployment, Candace is on a mission to help other people bounce back. Using insightful stories with uplifting inspirational songs, Candace's thought-provoking programs provide real life applications. Meet Candace and enjoy a program song and lyrics at www.RelentlessResilience.com.

You Do Your Job, I'll Do Mine

Kaylan Daane

LIFE IS LIKE A ROLLER COASTER OF UPS and downs. We all have different experiences but similar paths. I'll share with you a few snippets from my life that shaped me, and reveal the wisdom I've learned from all of it.

One-tenth of a Second

At fourteen, I am on both the swim team and the tennis team. I miss qualifying for the 1960 Olympic Trials in swimming by one-tenth of a second. God, I wish I had missed it by more! This one inspired moment, in which I swam the race of my life, haunts my parents for the rest of their lives. Mom keeps retelling the story to everyone while quickly thrusting her hand forward, simulating the quicker touch that would have ignited my career as an Olympian athlete.

I am expected to swim the same, or faster, in every race, and I never equal, or beat, that one historic breaststroke swim. Coaches scrutinize my breaststroke form and make changes to my arm stroke and leg kick. My unorthodox frog kick is changed to look more normal. Four years later, at the 1964 Olympics, a faster "whip kick" is first used in place of the normal frog kick. Immediately I recognize it. That's what I had been doing naturally; it just hadn't been used yet by swimmers as far as we knew. It's the one thing that gave me a faster time, and the first thing the coaches changed. Sometimes the wrong things get altered.

One day Mom comes to me in tears. She tells me Dad has what his doctor calls depression, and he might kill himself. She says, "Mary Kay, your dad gets so happy when you work hard and swim faster. Do it for Dad, Mary Kay; that will be your job. I'll take care of all your other things." And I do my job by becoming a tennis star, because in those days fewer girls played competitive tennis, and I can easily beat almost any girl and a lot of boys. And Dad does his job by being pleased again with my accomplishments, and doesn't kill himself.

Grandma's Apple Cider Rule

I'm seven and I try hard to keep the secrets between Grandma and me. It's one of her rules and the only way I stay alive when it's just the two of us at home. Also, if I tell Mom that Grandma does mean things to me, Mom stops me and with dutiful eyes says, "You have to understand, Mary Kay, Grandma is old." I scrunch up my face into a pitiful pout and yell, "I don't understand! Grandma's always been old; it's not fair!" It's true: Grandma was already a mean eighty when I was born.

Tonight Mom's at a teacher's meeting, Dad's at a council meeting, and Grandma's on the attack the moment they leave. She tells me to do something different from what Mom just told her I'm supposed to do. Grandma does this a lot. Tonight I'm having a friend spend the night, and Grandma starts yelling at me, "Call her and tell her she can't come over!" When I say no, Grandma explodes into a raging combination of crying and yelling. "You're mean to your grandma! I'm going to kill myself and you'll be sorry. Your mom and dad will hate you for doing this to me." She stomps up the stairs heading to the little porch off of the second floor hallway. I run up after her only to see her with one leg over the railing yelling, "I'm going to end this suffering you put me through!"

I don't want her to die, but I'm scared to get close; she might throw me over instead. I huddle in the other corner of the porch, begging and crying for her not to jump. I'm gasping for air. I feel I'm passing out and I won't be able to stop her from killing herself. Breathing is now impossible between my large gasps and violent sobbing. I am terrified!

I don't remember Grandma coming off the railing, but there she is, right in front of me. I stare into her pleading, scared eyes, which I've never seen before. Wow! She's afraid to hurt me when I'm sick.

I now know what to do when it gets scary: just get sick! I feel strong knowing this, so when Mom and Dad come home I tell them the "secret" of what happened tonight with Grandma.

The next day I'm off to school wearing my new Brownie uniform. I come home, and as usual pour myself a glass of apple cider. As I raise my glass to take a sip, Grandma's hand comes across my face and knocks the juice glass right out of my hands. Mom rushes in as I'm looking down at the streaks on my new Brownie shirt. I hear Mom saying, "You should thank your Grandmother, Mary Kay. She just saved your life. You almost drank lye and it would have killed you!"

Weird! Grandma keeps lye in the basement and uses it to make soap. What's it doing up here? Where's my apple cider? Mom says the two bottles look alike. I look at Grandma. Her lips are tightly smiling. The message is clear: "I can take you out anytime!"

I'll always remember Grandma's Apple Cider Rule: "Don't tell the secrets or I'll take you out!" This is a promise from Grandma – signed, sealed, and delivered in a very dangerous way. Mom knows this danger, too; that's why she told me what to say to Grandma. I'm numb and feel like a robot as I mechanically say, "Thank you, Grandma, for saving my life."

It's almost January in Minnesota, and I'm sitting on the little second floor porch, naked in the snow, trying to get pneumonia. This is the best way to feel safe, but I'm having trouble making myself sick, so I learn to fake it. I hold the thermometer against my lamp's light bulb until it hits a scary number. The doctor arrives and puts me in the hospital under observation. Here I discover my most wonderful place ever; everyone is nice and I feel safe and protected all night. "Being in the hospital is the best!" I think.

What I've Learned along the Way

I've learned you don't have to have bruises to have been abused. This big "aha" moment came to me when I was forty-five years old and halfway through an *Oprah Winfrey Show*. Thank you, Oprah! You filled in the edges around my jigsaw puzzle so I could fit together the rest of the pieces.

I was taught it's my responsibility to keep others happy and safe by giving them things they want to have from me. I had to keep myself safe by pretending, lying, being good in sports, and keeping the family secrets. I have since learned this wasn't my job, but when I was just a kid it was a smart thing to do.

I was taught that if a person didn't like me, it was my fault. If someone told me they loved my bright shining eyes, I'd make it a point to have them shining even brighter the next time they saw me. I learned these were smart things to do as a kid in order to survive, but as I started going through ups and downs on the journey to becoming an adult, I found I didn't know who "I" was; I had become a people pleaser to remain safe.

As an adult, I found some relief through pills and alcohol; they seemed to bury some of the feelings that were painful. Sometimes I thought I had found answers after four or five drinks or two or three pills, but the insights were fleeting the morning after. Eventually, years later, after becoming clean and sober, after surviving cancer and a stroke, I learned it was time to go on a journey to discover myself.

I've been sober thirty-seven years now. What I learned was that I had to put away for good many of the behaviors I used as a child to survive. Just like an alcoholic needing relief with a drink, I couldn't bring them back, not even to use them one more time. My lying, pretending, and creating illnesses had become habits, and I was addicted to how they got me out of doing things I didn't want to do without making anyone mad. If I find myself using a crutch that I need to put away for good, I now immediately tell the truth and come clean. This takes away the reason I use many of my crutches, which is to feel the relief the habit has brought me in the past. I try not to be hard on myself for reaching back to old habits that I have put away for good, but what I do with those feelings is so important. When I take steps to delay myself from acting on my desire to drink, for example, I grow stronger with each step I take, and it can be the difference between a quality life and death.

What I've also learned along the way is to be loving, kind, forgiving, and gentle with myself — exactly what I wanted others to be to me when I was a child. "Keep what is worth keeping and then — with the breath of kindness — blow the rest away." This is from *A Life for a Life* by Dinah Maria Mulock Craik.

I've learned there are some very hard lessons I can't just gently blow away. I'll need to walk through them, even if it puts me through hell or I end up at ground zero financially. For a period of two years many of these hard lessons came at me all at once, but I got stronger with each step I took, and I wouldn't trade them for the world. I find I'm now strong, honest, and can stand up for myself. I've found a very important part of me that's worth keeping and is a perfect fit in my puzzle of life.

I've learned our minds are powerful creators. I became very good at creating illness, but it became too dangerous to continue, so I had to put it away. In 1972, at twenty-six, I had one of the happiest days of my life: I gave birth to our son. Three days later, I was given a less-than-one-percent chance of living. The doctors hadn't known I had ovarian cancer, and the cyst exploded inside me days after we brought our son home. My mom ran around getting me the best doctors at the Mayo Clinic in Rochester, Minnesota, and I was flown there by medical plane. I started receiving loving support from friends, family, doctors, and nurses. Up to that point I had just gone numb, probably from all the drugs I was receiving. But then I came around and got angry. I hung in there and received as a gift a deep gratitude such as I've never felt before. I had a beautiful baby boy at home, my first child, and I was so grateful for him and so much in my life. I started praying to God and, yes, promising so many things I'd do if only I would live. As a child I was used to bargaining for my life.

It was prayer, intention, and visioning that prompted the right things to show up at the right moments, from the right doctors to an experimental drug to miracles. I underwent surgery and had radioactive phosphorus poured into me. New pictures of my baby boy were sent to me every day. I gave one last quick and simple prayer, followed by one more promise to never smoke cigarettes, and then I just let all of it go. Something I don't exactly understand and can't describe happened; something more powerful than I took control of my life for me. I felt calmness and knew that my only job was to follow the directions given to me by medical experts, set my intentions, hold my visions, and express my gratitude. This knowledge came from a place deep inside me that knew my intentions and desires.

I've been cancer-free for forty-two years. Getting sick is something I still work on putting away for good. I used to wonder when I got sick if I had caused it with my thinking, or if sometimes shit just happens. Maybe it's partly the consequences of years of tension and trying to get sick catching up with me, but I've let go of needing to know the why. My job is to create the intentions and visions of what I want in my life, and I want health!

Right now I'm setting the intention of putting away for good my eating of excess foods that are not good for me but temporarily make me feel better. My weight has been yo-yoing up and down for years, and I still can't understand why I do it. But then, I don't need to know why in order to change the behavior, do I?

I know that it's important to say "Yes" to what you want to see in your life, even if it's way beyond your safe boundaries, scares you, and doesn't feel good. That's the process of your starting to get to your truth, and in the end it will set you free.

So I say…
 "Yes" to being a writer.

"Yes" to taking the plunge and putting what's been in my head onto paper.

"Yes" to telling my secrets.

"Yes" to the person out there who thinks they are alone; who doesn't feel normal and wonders what normal looks like; who doesn't feel safe and free and wants that above all else; who tries to find the answers through living a secret life in their head and looking into lit homes at night to see how "normal" families live.

"Yes" to finally lighting my own windows with words on the pages, so you can peer into my life. If you get goose bumps or an "aha" moment, you'll recognize parts of my story that might be true for you, too. Know that you're not alone and that you can survive and prosper beyond what you ever can imagine. You can accomplish dreams you have not yet dared to dream. Know that I'm here for you, that I love you, and that at any age you can create a brilliant life and light up your own windows for someone else.

There's one last thing. If you're tired of hearing past ghosts calling you by your name, it's okay to choose another name. That's how I became Kaylan Daane.

According to doctors, **Kaylan Daane** shouldn't even be alive. She has survived and thrived through many life challenges including abuse without bruises, alcoholism, financial challenges, one-tenth of a second from Olympic Trials, cancer, and more. Kaylan is a walking testament to the fact that we're never alone and that we can survive and prosper at any age. Learn more about Kaylan and get your free gift at www.KaylanDaane.com.

A Gift in Disguise

Lynn Finley

"In order to know the light, we must first experience the darkness."
~ Carl Jung

January 12th, 2012

I PACED BACK AND FORTH IN MY OFFICE waiting for the phone to ring, waiting for the call. What was he going to say? Would he tell me everything was going to be okay? I had never been so scared in all my life. My office began to feel bigger as I could feel myself getting smaller and swallowed up by its enormity. I could hear faint voices down the hall indicating life was continuing on despite the fact that mine felt like it was standing still.

The phone rang and my heart skipped a beat. I could see my doctor's phone number appear in the caller ID. My voice trembled as I answered hello. He told me to come to his office. I knew then it couldn't be good.

When I arrived at my doctor's office, I was promptly ushered into a waiting room. He walked in with a forced smile on his face. In the instant he uttered the words "Lynn, you have breast cancer," my heart sank. It felt like someone had just punched me in the gut. Could this really be happening to me? How could I have breast cancer? It didn't even run in my family. Is this how I'm going to die? Will I see my twin boys graduate from high school? In that very moment my life took a 180-degree turn from normal to not knowing anything for certain anymore.

My husband and I met with the surgeon a few days later. He told me he'd perform a lumpectomy on my left breast and he didn't think it would be much of an issue. But first he wanted me to take several tests. The first test and probably the most grueling was the MRI. I had to lay face down, motionless, with my breasts hanging through two holes, for over an hour. After the MRI was complete I could tell there was something wrong by the look on the technician's face. He looked very sad for me. After the MRI there were x-rays, blood tests, more biopsies, and the scariest of all… a PET scan. There I sat, in the hospital where I gave birth to my two sons many years before when I felt my life was ahead of me, and now I felt my life was behind me and I was closer to its end.

At the time I was working for a big entertainment company in a senior-level position, and had been there for twenty-plus years. When I found out I had breast cancer, I told my boss and we cried in my office. I had known this man since I had been twenty-four years old – a mere child. I thought he cared about me. Little did I know at the time that that was the last time we would ever speak.

"A true measure of a man is how he treats someone who
can do him absolutely no good."
~ Dr. Samuel Johnson

After the biopsy, the nurse told me to keep an ice pack in my bra and go home and take it easy, but I just smiled and headed back to the office. My job was so stressful and demanding that I felt it was more important to go back to work than to go home and take care of myself. My job was still more important than me at that point. Walking back through the halls of the office was surreal. I felt like I was in slow motion, like I was in a movie playing a role of someone other than myself. People talked, but I really didn't hear what they said. There I sat, in a meeting, with an ice pack in my bra, listening to the meaningless chatter that poured out of my colleagues' mouths, and all the while all I could think was, *Somebody please wake me from this nightmare.*

When I returned to my surgeon's office three weeks later after all the tests were complete, I noticed he had a different look on his face than on the first day we had met. The first time he looked hopeful and optimistic. Now he grimaced and looked like he was in pain. He continually shook his head, saying, "I don't like what I saw." I realized something wasn't right. He looked at me and said, "Lynn, you have breast cancer in both breasts. I am recommending you have a bilateral mastectomy." Huh? What? What just happened? How did I go from a lumpectomy to save my breast to a bilateral mastectomy to now save my life in such a short period of time? Isn't that a little drastic? I was in shock. I could not contain my fear and anxiety. I was a mess. I left the office with swollen eyes and a prescription for Xanax. My husband was working that day, and since I didn't want to tell him the news over the phone, I waited until he got home. I hadn't cried that hard since the day my father had died. I sobbed so much I felt sick to my stomach.

The bilateral mastectomy and reconstruction were scheduled three weeks after the completion of the testing. During that time I felt like cancer was coursing through my body with a vengeance. Every ache or pain I had, I assumed it was cancer spreading throughout my body. The fear was intense and overwhelming. The surgery would be three days after my fiftieth birthday – certainly not what I expected when I imagined turning fifty. I did not tell many people for several reasons. Every time I uttered the words, I burst into tears and it became more painful and more real. I didn't want to be defined by the cancer. And I didn't want people feeling sorry for me. I just wanted to crawl in a hole and wake up after it was all over. But I had a long road of recovery and healing ahead of me.

The day of the surgery will be forever etched in my mind. I was consumed with fear and anxiety. I really didn't think I was going to come out of that hospital alive. I watched my husband appear helpless and struggling to hold back his tears as they wheeled me away through the cold, bright, sterile hallway. I thought it was the last time I would see him.

I awoke in the most excruciating pain, and lay there for several hours without pain medication because they didn't have a room for me. But I was very much aware and relieved that I was alive.

A week after the surgery I got the courage to remove the bandages. I was so scared of what I was going to find – as if I were some sort of Frankenstein. As I stood in front of the mirror, I pulled away the bandages. I was shocked and horrified and fell to my knees and wept when I saw the mutilation. I felt horribly disfigured. What happened? And so the tears began and continued for a very long time. It truly is an emotional disease.

The PET scan that had been performed weeks earlier revealed a mass on my ovary, so one month after my double mastectomy I went in for a complete hysterectomy. The anesthesia and the surgery left me nauseous, depressed, and in full-blown menopause. I was still in a lot of pain from the mastectomy and the expanders. Months later I looked back in my notes and saw that I journaled, "Why did they bother saving me? I wish I would have died." I really felt like I had hit rock bottom. I spent most of my days crying from the moment I woke up to the moment I went to bed.

Prior to this illness I had always been sick. Sinus infections, bronchitis, shingles – you name it. My job was literally making me sick. It's no wonder that all that resentment and anger materialized as breast cancer. To make matters worse, while I was on disability dealing with my health, not only was my job given to someone else but my office was cleared out and all my belongings packed and hauled away without my knowledge. Some people reached out to my husband in fear that I had died. Why else would the office be cleared out? This was truly hurtful and devastating. How could someone who had given twenty-plus years of loyal service to a company be treated so horribly during their darkest hour? Thrown out and discarded. One would think that in my situation things would have been different with my employer, that they would have had empathy… a heart. Needless to say, I was not in the happiest place on earth.

I found myself on many occasions praying and asking for guidance and to be shown the way. One could say the diagnosis was the "tap on the shoulder" I needed to make a lifestyle change, but that would be an understatement. I guess all the smaller illnesses were the taps on the shoulder that I ignored. The breast cancer was the final baseball bat to the head – the infamous "wake up call." I asked to be shown the way, but didn't expect or imagine it to show up in that form.

As the fog lifted and I started to feel a little better, the crying was less frequent and I had a yearning for information and guidance. I was drawn to books by Wayne Dyer, Deepak Chopra, Eckhart Tolle, Louise Hay, and Anita Moorjani, to name a few. I joined a cancer support center where they offered services to help in recovery and healing, such as Reiki, Qi Gong, meditation, and hypnotherapy. I met other survivors who became some of my biggest healers of all. One of my healers told me to picture myself as a little girl, one who dreamed of growing breasts and having children. She told me to reach out to that little girl and tell her it was going to be okay; that I loved her and that I was there for her.

Coincidentally, the day before that I had found a picture of myself as a little girl about eight years old on vacation in Lake George, New York. I had a sad facial expression, one we called "boo-boo lip." When I was told to picture myself as a little girl, I immediately thought of that picture. Visualizing myself as that little girl was very powerful. It made me realize how very sad I was and how much she (I) needed to be nurtured and cared for. I started to visualize that sad little girl in the picture reaching her hand up to what appeared to be God. As that hand led her, she looked up and her boo-boo lip turned into a smile.

This visualization helped me through a very dark time. The more I visualized this, the more I felt I wasn't alone.

I also began spending more time in nature. I put on my music and watched the leaves of the trees dance in the wind. I became keenly aware of all the beauty around me: the waves hitting the beach, the sand in between my toes, the smell of eucalyptus, the sounds of the birds. My senses were heightened and I felt an awakening of my spirit. My tears were no longer tears of pain and sadness, but rather tears of joy. I felt bathed in warmth and light in the center of my being... my soul. I was finally experiencing joy, and I had never felt so alive.

I was opening up my mind, my heart, and my soul. I realized that in every step of this journey I was meeting my healers. They came in all shapes and sizes. One step led to the next, and all were filled with synchronicities. There were people who healed me with their love, their friendship, their wisdom, their guidance, their healing touch, their spirituality, and so on. A new world had opened up for me. Had this world been there all along and I just hadn't seen it?

When I was set to return to work, I was offered a "like" position, but would still be in the same department working for the same people who didn't care if I had lived or died several months prior. This weighed heavily on my heart. The once compassionate, empathetic, family-friendly workplace was a thing of the past. How could I go back there? I had let the job become who I was and I had let it define me. But the truth was, that was not who I was at all.

The cancer actually defined me more than that job ever had. I never thought I could survive without it, but the real question was how could I survive with it? I spent a lot of time praying and quieting my mind to find the answer. When I imagined myself not returning, I experienced a sense of joy. It felt right. I truly believe one door has to close for another to open. The golden handcuffs no longer served me. I decided to not return, and I continue to experience joy and happiness like never before. And I am healthier than I have ever been. I think my fountain of youth has come from my happiness and my new awareness and awakening.

I worry about my "default personality" emerging and going back to my old ways, but my awareness of this helps me get back on track. I'm still healing, and some days are easier than others. I love my meditation music and listening to it while I hike in the mountains. I laugh constantly. I feel like I see life as a child, and that brings more meaning to everything I see and feel. I released control and my attachment to the outcome of events – a very liberating process. I try to practice forgiveness. What I've come to learn about forgiveness is that it's not about letting the person off the hook; it's about feeling at peace. It's a gift you give yourself.

What I began to realize was that I might actually have a few good years ahead of me... maybe even thirty or more. I have an opportunity to live my life differently. This huge event in my life did not occur for me to continue to live life as I had in the past, as that obviously wasn't working for me. I could choose to feel sad, depressed, and a victim, or I could choose to be happy. I choose happy.

What I have learned is that once you let go and give in to the universe, to God, you will be at peace. Operate from your heart and soul, not from your head. Let life unfold, and know that you are where you need to be and that you have everything you need. You are divinely guided.

"If you are depressed, you are living in the past. If you are anxious, you are living in the future. If you are at peace, you are living in the present."

~ Lao Tzu

A New York native, at twenty-four **Lynn Finley** moved to Los Angeles where she worked for a major entertainment company for twenty-two years. When a breast cancer diagnosis turned her life upside down, her priorities underwent a major shift and finding a new sense of purpose and higher calling is what she now embraces. Lynn's interest lies in coaching cancer survivors to discover a renewed life of joy and hope. Visit www.LynnMFinley.com for more information.

A Vital Shift: From Inner Child to Inner Captain

Lara Homans

My words are simple.
My heart is open.
My soul is ready to meet your eyes.

I HAVE NEVER TOLD ANYONE WHAT I KEPT inside in my heart and my mind for many years. I have never been brave enough to share the story about the little girl living inside me. This girl, falling in love with the sun and light, journeys and discoveries, miracles and stories, looks at the outer world with an endless curiosity. She tells me simple stories from my life whenever I need help, inspiration, courage, and confidence. I am writing this chapter with her words, her images, and her love. Though I have been keeping this little girl in my inner world since I can remember, I discovered the vital role of her presence only several years ago.

Feeding a Pain

I am the youngest child in my family. Large families were commonplace in the former Soviet Union after World War II. However, in our family there was a special reason for many children. My father badly wanted a son. After four girls, finally a boy was born. "Mission accomplished," my parents probably thought. Three years later my mother was surprised: she was pregnant again. What to do? I can only imagine what a difficult time she had, but for the first time in her life my mother decided to have an abortion.

So one early morning when my mother was almost ready to go to the hospital for the procedure, she couldn't find her medical card and test results. Then her eldest daughter came to her, hugged her, and said quietly, "Mom, we burned your papers." And the second daughter added, "Let this child be." Mom sat down on the sofa and began to cry. My sisters were so proud when they later told me about what they had done! "You should be grateful to us for being born."

Is a child's heart strong enough to accept such a harsh pain? This pain appeared at one moment and remained forever in my life: "I am an unwanted child." Over many years this story became my permanent burden. It influenced and determined my personality, my character, and my entire life.

"My son is the sense of my life," said my father to me one day. He probably said this without thinking. I was almost seventeen years old, and asked him, "How about your daughters? How about me?" And I added, "I didn't ask anyone to bring me into this world!" I slammed the door and ran out of the house. Choking with tears and unspoken resentment, I was mentally repeating, "I am an unwanted child."

Many years have passed since then, but I have not forgotten that story. Whenever I met the eyes of other people I was always looking for their approval, recognition, acceptance, and love. During the years my hidden story (I am an unwanted child) learned how to show up in different ways.

I managed to accomplish a lot in my life, professionally and personally. I graduated from secondary school and received a gold medal for outstanding scholastic achievement for ten years of schooling. While a student living in Ukraine, I went to work in Siberia for a summer to earn money to help my parents pay off their old debt. I obtained two university degrees. I became one of the pioneering professionals in public relations in Ukraine, my home country. I developed a successful career, and along with my colleagues received an outstanding award from the World Bank.

I worked hard at my job, first to convince my family – and then to convince others – that it was worth it to have me around. Willingness to be accepted, recognized, and rewarded became a major focus of my life.

Finding a Peace

One time when I was visiting my parents during a short summer vacation, an incredible moment happened. After having lunch, my mother lay down on the couch to relax a little bit. I sat on the floor and put my head on her lap. She started quietly talking about something that I had never been brave enough to ask her about.

"My dear girl, I never told you about it… From the day you were born you brought me strength, energy, and hope. I looked at you sleeping in your cradle and prayed to God to give me enough health so I could see you going to the first grade, see you graduating, and then see you as a beautiful bride and later as a happy wife. Most of all I wanted to live up to the moment when your kids would call me Grandma. I call you my little angel," said my mom.

At that moment a wave of tenderness and warmth came over me. I was scared to move. I was afraid to embrace what I had just heard. I never doubted that my mother wanted me to be here. I never blamed her for making a decision that my sisters effectively ended up canceling. Though, when I was thinking about my father in the context of that story, I felt an old and acute pain in my heart. I always had a strong and painful resentment towards him when I remembered the words about a sense of his life. At the same time I always wanted to deserve his attention and recognition. I always wanted to win his love.

Seven years ago I read Debbie Ford's books *The Dark Side of the Light Chasers* and *The Secret of the Shadow* about a phenomenon she called the Shadow Belief. My Shadow Belief around which I created my Shadow Story is being an unwanted child. Shadow Beliefs can define our lives; we are committed to these stories from our past. We create Shadow Stories unconsciously in order to build a defense against painful experiences with which we could not cope during childhood, and which we often do not know how to cope with in adulthood.

During a Shadow Workshop that I was taking part in, Debbie asked me two questions: "What gift does your story hold for you? Why can you be grateful for your story?" *How is it possible to be thankful for the pain that lived in my heart for so many years?* I asked myself. These questions became a turning point in my life. I started realizing that I still needed to face my own Shadow Story – consciously, gracefully, and openly, with a long-standing resentment and hidden pain – and find its true meaning.

Opening the hidden wisdom of my story did not come immediately. It took time, energy, and courage to reframe my past and present. First I had to accept the initial story as a fact. Then I learned how to forgive my parents, especially my father, for divulging "the truth about my birth." Last, I had to do my own inner work to find a new meaning for my story instead of being poisoned by the old one.

One bright, sunny afternoon in early May of 2011, I was sitting on the waterfront in San Diego looking at the distant horizon merging with the azure sky and the ocean. For the first time in my life, and in spite of knowing that he would be unable to read my words, I wrote a letter to my late father. My father, whom I loved and feared at the same time; whom I respected and valued for a strong character and a kind heart; whom I was gravitating to and running from; from whom I was hiding my dreams and thoughts; and from whom I was waiting for recognition of my skills and achievements. In a recent meditation I had surprisingly seen him as a little boy who had not received enough love and appreciation from his own family.

I asked him about the belated forgiveness – for my long-standing grudge, coldness, detachment, reluctance, and unwillingness to open my heart; for my inability to be a truly caring daughter; for all my unspoken gratitude – he did so much for me!

A series of memorable moments flashed in my mind…

My father raising me up in the air while I was sitting on a small chair. It was my seventh birthday, and, per family tradition, he helped me "fly to the sky" seven times…

His knocking on the door of my room in the student dormitory. He had brought a baked chicken and a sack of recently harvested potatoes from home for me…

Another time he was holding on his lap my only daughter, his youngest granddaughter, named after my mother…

One heartbreaking day he was hugging me and crying with me – he understood and shared my pain, as six years before he had lost his wife, my mother, and two days before I had just lost my husband.

With sincere words of forgiveness, gratitude, and boundless light and love, I was letting go of my old pain. I was re-experiencing the joy and care that had been hidden from my awareness in the shadow of my story.

Being willing to earn attention, approval, acceptance, and love, first from the closest people in the family and then from other people in different life contexts, helped me become the person I am now. I learned to be sensitive to relationships, and to feel and understand other people's emotions. I learned to accept people as they are and see in others hidden, unrealized abilities; and most important, to see the inner child who lives in each of us.

My old childhood story began getting a new meaning, but the most valuable awareness was still waiting for me to discover.

Bridging a Fear and a Faith

In August of 2011, together with my second husband, I went to Dark Harbor, Maine, where his mother lived. Surrounded by a new extended family, I celebrated my forty-ninth birthday. That bright afternoon I was sitting on a sun-warmed dock observing the passing sailboats and distant ships. My inner weather contrasted with the warm and shiny weather outside.

I thought that a major part of my life was over. Professionally I had accomplished a lot, but for some reason I was not feeling satisfied, neither with the present moment of my life nor with my past successes. What did I want to do in the future? What did I really want to achieve in my life? What was my destiny? These questions scared me and made my heart ache.

If I had said to my husband, siblings, colleagues, and friends that I had lost my identity and was feeling a strong emotional bankruptcy inside, they would have been surprised. They probably would not have understood me at all, especially given what I had accomplished up to that point. I was working for well-known international and Ukrainian organizations where I was respected for my experience, dedication, perseverance, and ability to work hard. There were good opportunities for advancement.

So what was making me cry, sitting on the wooden jetty staring at the silver-blue distance and the beautiful boats?

In my childhood I saw ships only as pictures in books. But that didn't prevent me, as a little girl, from dreaming of being the captain of a big, beautiful, white ship. I imagined how I would stand on the captain's bridge, looking through binoculars, keeping the steering wheel straight. I wanted to sail my ship far away, see distant lands, meet new people, and speak different languages.

I had come to this small island in Maine for family reasons. Might there be another purpose to be there now? Maybe Dark Harbor was a catalyst, allowing me to finally choose a new route in my life, especially professionally.

A few years before I had left the corporate sector, started creating new training and consultancy programs, and began investing in myself as a coach. But even while doing this I wasn't sure I had enough strength, life time, and, mainly, courage to follow my new professional path fully. I was still scared to go far away from my previous and well-known "professional land."

On August 12th, 2011, I wrote in my diary these words: "The next year and all following ones I will live as the Captain of My Life." To be honest, I didn't know how to do this, but I wanted it. I manifested it and I was ready for challenging changes. On that wonderful afternoon I began a new amazing journey that continues today. I am sure I had been preparing for this journey my whole life.

I was blessed by the chance to meet Debbie Ford, read many of her books, and participate in a one-year integrative coaching program taught by her and her colleagues. Finally I had found a true passion and a vivid purpose for my life. As in my childhood, I started again writing and sharing my stories. Now they are for adults who want to connect various dots – events, experiences, openings – in their personal and professional lives; who want to find their true paths, especially when they have already made and crossed many roads.

Now I am a Transformational Story Coach. I help people discover, accept, learn, and love their transformational self-journeys.

Today "we" stand on the captain's bridge of my life ship together – the seasoned woman who has already experienced a lot in her life and continues to discover important things about herself, people, and the world, and the little girl who was able to hold courage, gratitude, passion, and love for me. What unites us? A loving heart, open soul, curious mind, skillful hands, and the willingness to live fully.

The little girl is named Loving Lara. She managed to do an incredible thing – to wait patiently until I finally understood an obvious truth.

I have long been accepted and loved by my family. The only person who was scared to see, accept, and love this little girl was myself. My little inner child is wise to help me discover true meaning, real purpose, and enduring values for my life. She patiently teaches me to believe strongly and love unconditionally, to wonder about the simple things joyfully, to dream boldly, to work constantly, and to make dreams happen. She is my little angel. She is my inner light that shines every moment of my life. She is a source of energy and love who transformed into the words you are reading now. She has been a blessing my entire life.

Remember that day I said to my father, "I didn't ask anyone to bring me into this world"? I was so wrong! I begged to come here! I am so grateful to my father and mother, my sisters and my brother, my inner child and my fate, and the Divine and Highest Force that created me, for letting me come HERE!

I deeply believe that every story matters. And my story I just shared with the world matters, too. There was a vital reason for me to be born, wasn't there?

Lara Homans found her life's passion and new professional path after spending twenty years in business communications. Through an in-depth, self-discovering journey she learned how to find, accept, and transform painful life stories into healing and inspiring ones. She became a Transformational Story Coach, and now helps seasoned women find an inner source of vital and creative energy by learning, loving, and leading their life stories. To get her free story-coaching session, please visit www.LaraHomans.com.

If Only…

Linda Hyden

ARE YOU TIRED OF THE DAILY STRUGGLES of not feeling that you are enough… not good enough, smart enough, pretty enough, successful enough, rich enough, creative enough, thin enough, or educated enough? Are you ready to transform your life by understanding and accepting that you are unique and **wonderfully made** by God to serve a purpose that only you can fulfill with your life? If you answered yes, then please start right now by getting rid of your "not enoughs" and finding and living your unique life purpose!

It took me a long time to accept that I was enough (just the way I am) and that I was exactly the way God intended me to be. I was a chubby elementary student, an overweight junior high student, and a fat high school student. My weight topped out at over two hundred-twenty pounds when I was a sophomore in high school. At five foot six inches tall, I was indeed obese.

Because of my weight I looked different from the average kid in school. I was an easy target for jokes, jeers, and taunts because of my weight, and many kids and adults made fun of me. I was also shy and introverted. I felt things deeply, internalized the nasty comments made to me, did nothing outwardly to defend myself or deflect the taunts, and by the time I was eight years old I believed that there was something very wrong with me because I was fat. Not only did I believe that something was off-kilter with me, but I also felt that being fat meant I had done something wrong.

I was a cute, chubby little eight-year-old girl with dark hair cut by my father into a pixie cut (using the bowl-on-the-head technique), wearing clothes my grandmother made for me because it was hard for my mommy to find clothes that fit me. I was also smart, sensitive, intuitive, musically inclined, and scared to death of people and life. I often wonder if food would have remained such a battle for me if when I was little I'd had someone in my life to help me see the good things (truths) about "Little Linda." But I learned early that I was not enough, and I began to loathe my body. I was not pretty enough, thin enough, smart enough, popular enough, or cute enough. I didn't understand why I was different, but I knew I was. Being different meant I was *not* like my friends at school, and that was a bad thing.

I learned at a young age that being overweight meant people felt they had the right – even those who did not know me – to make comments, joke, and taunt me. One day when I was twelve, I was playing with friends at a neighbor's house. Their hundred-year-old grandmother (or so she seemed) lived with them. She was known for speaking her mind and saying what she thought. I went into the house to have lunch with my friends, walked through the living room where Grandma sat in her rocker as usual, smiled at her, and she said to me, "Honey, don't you know that shirt makes you look as big as the side of a barn? You should never wear stripes running horizontally because they make you look fatter than you already are. Now you don't want that, do you?" To this day I remember that shirt and how hurt I felt when Grandma said those things to me. I loved that shirt! It had bright-colored stripes and I thought I looked great in it. I was finally getting some boobs and the shirt made me feel pretty, at least until that moment.

For as long as I can remember people have made fun of my weight and how I look. By the time I hit high school I had learned to be prepared for taunting, name calling, denigrating remarks, and snide comments. One day when I was going up the wrong way on the high school stairs trying to get to a class in a hurry, a group of boys shouted, "Open up! Here comes Wide Track. It's Wide Track coming through." Another favorite taunt by the boys was "Tubby, Tubby, two by four, couldn't fit through the bathroom door, so she did it on the floor… turned around and did some more." I hurt so bad each time one of those things happened, and it reinforced in my mind that I was not enough and would never be enough.

Sometimes the insults and ridicule were more subtle, but just as hurtful. At lunch I would hear students say, "No wonder she is so fat. Look at what she is eating." I then developed a habit of skipping lunch and "closet eating." High school signaled the beginning of dieting for me. One day in ninth grade civics class the guy who sat across from me (his name was Alan and I thought he was such a dreamboat) looked directly at my mouth and said, "Man, the inside of your lips are even fat!" I didn't smile for weeks! Sometimes the hurtful comments came from adults. During band camp one summer, one of the band mothers who volunteered with the uniforms said to me, "Honey, I'm not sure we have anything big enough to fit you." I was devastated!

As I grew older and traveled my spiritual path to heal my wounds and get to know the person God made me to be, I learned a lot of lessons; lessons that I now use to help other women get healthy spiritually, emotionally, and physically; lessons that help you learn to love the skin you are in, move past the hurts that keep you stuck, and love deeply by forgiving yourself and others, all so you can make the unique contribution to this world that only you can make.

I'd like to share with you two life lessons I've learned. The first is about the *not-enough/if-only* condition. Millions of women suffer from the not-enough/if-only condition and find that it monopolizes their thoughts and actions. This condition is the agony we suffer daily when we feel that we are not good enough, smart enough, pretty enough, successful enough, rich enough, thin enough, educated enough… and the list goes on. And then we wish or pray the "if only" prayer. "If only,

Lord, I could be smarter, more successful, richer, thinner, prettier, etc., then I'd be so much happier; life would be good and I could do more good in this world."

The causes of the condition are unique and personal to each of us. My not-enough/if-only condition was birthed in me at the young age of eight when I learned that being fat made me different, and different was bad. Not all women struggle with body image. Some are weighed down by other things in their lives that keep them stuck and unhappy. If you have already been to counseling and know what your issues are, that is an excellent start. Indicators that you suffer from this condition include things like stressed family relationships; unhealthy friendships; bad habits like uncontrolled shopping, unhealthy sexual relations, and alcohol or drug misuse and abuse; uncontrolled anger; having unreal expectations of yourself or others; and unhealthy stress related to work, home, church, and social obligations that are unbalanced or have gone awry.

Every one of us who suffers from the not-enough/if-only condition has at least one thing in common: we learned somewhere along our life journey that something about us was different, which meant there was something wrong or bad about us. We believed the lies we were told; they became our truth and defined our lives. Many of us have spent the better part of our lives trying to keep the world from seeing the real us for fear that everyone will then know (sure enough) that we are not enough.

For years I prayed, "If only I were thin, Lord. If I were thin, everything would be okay and my life would be so much better and happier. Lord, please let me lose one hundred pounds." "Lord, let me lose seventy pounds and then I will be enough." "Lord, it's me again. I still need to lose twenty pounds and then everything will be okay." I am a little embarrassed to admit this, but I used to wonder what people thought about if they weren't thinking about how bad their bodies looked or losing weight. I couldn't imagine what people spent their time thinking about if it wasn't weight or body image because those two things monopolized my time, my energy, my spirit, my life, my spending.

Women like me who suffer from low self-esteem and body-image issues don't think about our internal beauty because we are too caught up in disliking what we see in the mirror. I have actually coached a number of women who made one of their program goals to **not look** in the mirror when they passed by it. The mirror was a constant reminder of all their perceived flaws. Many of us spend an inordinate amount of time comparing ourselves to models and actresses, thus highlighting our flaws even further. I was never taught about internal beauty or different kinds of external beauty. I was never taught to question the logic of the stick-thin models of my era, or that people felt it was okay to humiliate and ridicule me for my weight. I was never told that being fat didn't make me a bad or weak person.

I learned during my healing journey that, like a diamond, your light needs to shine from within, and your inner light is the key to living a fulfilling life. When others look at you, the first thing they see may be your exterior body or the put-together package, but what they most often remember is the inner light that comes from your heart and soul. Just as a diamond intensifies the light that passes through it, you have the choice to intensify God's light that flows through you.

The second life lesson is the importance of finding and living your divine life purpose. How do you figure out your life purpose and how do you know if it is "right"? The first thing to get your arms around is that God loves you and has made you perfect and unique. Living your divine purpose is what makes you happy and brings joy to your life. Everyone deserves to be happy and find true joy in their life. Living your divine life purpose is the path to truly being the person you want to be.

Your purpose comes alive through your confidence and belief that it's the reason God placed you here on earth. Knowing your life purpose is great, but if you don't steadily take action towards living out that purpose, it is just a nice idea or thought. God wants to see action and outcomes. God gave us each a special life purpose because He views our lives as essential. What could be more important than getting up and going to work for the Lord every morning? Nothing! If you don't know how to set and work goals, learn how... now. Then talk to God; listen, listen, and listen for His answers; set your goals; and take action!

I promise if you pray and listen you will hear God's perfect will for your life. And don't worry about whether or not you are hearing Him correctly. He will direct and redirect your course. I used to tell my husband that I wished God would tell me exactly what I was supposed to do or be; that direction would make it so much easier and I'd be good to go. But we know that is not how God works. God wants us to take one step at a time, relying only on Him. He doesn't give us a complete road map, but rather gives us steps to take on our journeys. The Lord wants us to depend on Him, listen for Him, and have relationships with Him that include conversations like "Now Father, did I hear You correctly? You want me to do what?"

With lots of prayer and spiritual guidance I began to learn the truth about God's love for me and that my poor body image and low self-esteem were making it really hard to pursue my God-given purpose on this earth. As I healed I saw the awesome opportunity God was giving me to use what I had learned during my personal healing and spiritual growth to help other women do the same thing. The empowerment coaching program that was birthed from my personal healing experiences is called Life Doesn't Weight®. The results women are experiencing while applying the principles and techniques of Life Doesn't Weight® to their lives are amazing!

So are you ready to change? Have you had enough of living someone else's life and missing out on the awesome life that God intends for you? Are you tired of feeling inadequate and trying to keep the world from knowing the real you? Sometimes when you struggle with your self-image like I have for years it is hard to think beyond your insecurities and uncertainties. For the greater part of my life I believed the old negative voices playing in my head and bought in to the lies I was told. I have now learned how to heal old wounds that are keeping me stuck, set goals, love deeply by forgiving myself and others, and pursue my divine life purpose. It is time to move beyond the lies and find a new perspective on who God made you to be.

You are unique and *wonderfully made* by God to serve a purpose that only you can fulfil with your life. Make the decision today to allow your divine life purpose to be a blessing to others.

Linda Hyden, founder of Hyden Consulting, Inc., is a certified transformational coach, business owner, management consultant, and community leader whose God-given passion is to empower each woman to find her unique voice and make the special contribution to this world that only she can. Linda lives out this calling by coaching, consulting, leading, writing, and speaking. Visit her websites www.HydenConsulting.com and www.LifeDoesntWeight.com to see how she can help you transform your life.

Against All Odds:
From Pain to Possibility

Nisha Jackson

I SAT IN MY BEDROOM AS I HAD DONE so many times before, and listened to the familiar sounds of my mother cursing and running up the stairs in our apartment in the projects. My heart raced. I knew all too well what this meant. But I had no idea that the punishment of a seven-year-old for not washing the dishes clean would lead to the suffering I endured for years to come.

The door swung open with so much force that the knob dented the wall. I began to beg as I saw the all-too-familiar silhouette coming towards me holding that long whip of an extension cord. I was crouched down on the floor, holding my knees and rocking back and forth, with tears streaming down my face, and in a barely audible voice I heard that familiar faint whisper escape my lips: "Mommy, please..."

As in the past, this cry had no effect. It was actually a violation of our previous agreement about how I would take my punishment, and it only fueled her anger. She screamed, "Get over here and get on your knees!" I obeyed and slowly crawled toward her, one hand and one knee at a time, assumed the position on all fours, and hesitantly placed my head between her knees and felt the pressure on my head as her knees tightened. This was her remedy to keep me from running around the room and having to chase me to mete out my punishment.

I clenched my teeth to keep from screaming so the neighbors wouldn't hear me. I held my breath when I heard the whipping sound of the extension cord as it traveled through the air. The first landing of the cord on my rear was usually the worst. Today it was different. The whipping seemed to progress and last longer than before; her anger was fierce.

I crumpled to the floor when it ended, lay there in a fetal position, and silently sobbed. I listened as she ran my bath water. She returned to the door of my room and said, "Go take your bath." As she spoke, I recognized the all-too-familiar slur in her voice and saw her struggle to walk a straight line. This was a good sign, because it meant the drugs were taking effect and she would soon pass out.

As I was getting ready to get into the tub she did not leave the bathroom. Instead, she put the toilet seat down and began one of her talks about how hard her life was. I knew that I wasn't supposed to respond. It was best to just let her talk. But there was a problem this night; I could not sit in the bath water. It was too hot. I knew from the moment the bottom of my foot touched the water. I immediately pulled my foot out. This startled her and brought her attention to me. I whispered, "It's too hot."

She jumped up from the toilet, put me in the water, and held me down. I screamed and she put her hand over my mouth. I eventually stopped struggling. She told me to finish taking my bath and she went to bed. When she left I immediately put my feet on the sides of the tub out of the water. They were the most sensitive to the heat. I sat there, sobbing quietly, balancing on my rear, until I heard silence.

When I got out of the tub I was surprised to see that there were sores on my rear. I was scared because I didn't want my mother to see them. I hurried drying off and put my pajamas on and tiptoed to my bed. I slept on my stomach because the sores were turning into blisters.

The next morning I tried to get dressed for school, but to no avail. I peeked out of my bedroom trying to see if my mother was up. To my surprise, she was coming out of her room as I walked stiffly to the bathroom. She stopped me in the hallway and asked, "Why aren't you dressed?" I stood there frozen, staring at her, unable to move. She asked again and I mumbled, "My rear hurts." She told me to take my pajama pants down. I carefully put my hands inside the waistband to stretch it over the blisters and pulled them down. A look of panic crossed her face. She gasped, covered her mouth, and looked at me with fearful eyes.

She told me to go into my bedroom, and closed the door behind me. I didn't know what would happen next. I lay on my stomach in my bed with nothing covering my lower half. I heard her talking to someone on the phone. I waited all day, and when nighttime came and it was dark she came into my room with a towel, a needle, and a lighter. I watched in fear as she burned the needle with the lighter, tears streaming down my face. As she came close to my rear with the needle, I bit my lip and braced for the pain. Surprisingly, as she pierced the blisters, I didn't feel any pain. She pushed and dabbed the liquid that escaped with a gentleness that I had rarely seen. Then she left without our speaking a word.

Days passed; exactly how many, I'm not sure. During this time she would bring me food, but still neither of us uttered a word. One day I heard her outside yelling at the neighbors. Then I heard the most frightening sound that I could have imagined: a gunshot. I was scared and began to cry. I was torn between fear that my mother was dead and happiness that this could all be over.

As the sirens came closer I became anxious, wondering what would happen next. I heard voices and commotion outside. Then I heard the police searching the house, but I still was unable to find my voice. I stayed silent. Then it happened. I saw the knob turn slowly, and as I watched, my bedroom door creaked open. Two policemen entered the room, just like I'd seen them do in the movies. The first one entered and looked around the room, and then our eyes locked with each other. He asked if anyone else was in the room. I shook my head no. They came into the room, called for an ambulance, and just stared at my rear for a moment before asking my name. The ambulance came, and as they took me out I saw my mother in handcuffs.

The next six years were a whirlwind of events that included a long hospital stay in the burn ward, trials, therapist visits, and numerous foster homes. I was moved from foster home to foster home, due in part to a broken foster care system. Some of the homes shouldn't have been licensed. I was moved from others because my mother kept trying to get me back and would terrorize the families until they were scared for their safety. I became an experiment in a program they called "reunification." Periodically they would give me back to her to see if we could be reunited as a family. This always ended in abuse and my placement with another family.

At age eleven I was placed with my aunt, and for about two years my home life was stable. I thought this would be my home until I was eighteen, until one day when I was thirteen my mother came for a visit. My aunt had just returned home from the hospital, having had open heart surgery. My mother came over and started an argument. She and I began to fight. I tried to protect myself and my aunt, and I was willing to do anything in my power. Needless to say, a commotion occurred, and the police came and arrested my mother. My aunt said she was going to lie down for a bit while I went to take a bath. When I got out of the bathtub, I asked my aunt if she wanted me to turn off the television. There was no reply. I repeated the question more loudly, and when she didn't answer, I called the neighbor. He came over and told me she had died.

I was placed in Juvenile Hall for the weekend until they found a new foster home. I had not committed a crime, yet I was placed there because they couldn't find any temporary placement. Witnessing the scary crowd I was sharing this space with, my anger and hatred for my mother grew. The social worker came on Monday to transport me to my new placement. I had decided that it was now me against the world. I wanted no part of this system that had never protected me and always punished me.

On what seemed like the longest ride yet to a new foster home, but in actuality was only thirty minutes, I struggled with such questions as "How could God do this to me?" and "What have I done to deserve this?" I arrived at the new foster home, worn and bitter. I was rebellious. I did things that I was sure would get me kicked out of the home. I was mean and a force to be reckoned with.

Little did I know that I had been placed with a woman sent by God, who, though she was somewhat elderly, was willing to go toe to toe with us foster children to fulfill her purpose here on earth... and she did just that. She took in five teenaged girls from various problematic backgrounds and transformed them. She ruled with a loving, iron fist, and everyone knew of her in the neighborhood. They knew not to mess with her or any of her girls, but they also knew that if they needed anything she was the person they could trust.

She gave me little time to settle into my newly found rebelliousness. That day she sat me down and tried to find out where my head was. After numerous tries, she stopped trying to crack my exterior and told me what was expected of me in the home. She completed her discussion with the following: "When you're ready to talk, I'm here." There was so much caring, structure, and love from my new mother that I couldn't help but reluctantly settle in. I came to accept her as my mother.

When I was sixteen my biological mother was murdered. I now know that this was to be my final test and a turning point in my life. My foster mother sat me down and told me that my mother had died. My reply of "Good" caused her to squint one eye, which was a sign to us that she was going to pass on some much-needed wisdom, whether we wanted it or not. I still keep her words close to me today. She said, "I know that you have had rough beginnings, but she is still your mother and you must honor her with forgiveness! You cannot let her hold you captive! You have to forgive her in order to receive the blessings our God has in store for you."

There was much more to the wisdom she imparted, but finally she said, "The funeral is on Saturday. Don't let your grudge keep you out of heaven!" She then did what she normally did — walked past me and touched my shoulder as she left the room. I sat there trying my best to find a hole in her logic that I could cling to, but to no avail. I attended my mother's funeral that Saturday and struggled for some time after with "letting go and letting God" guide me in my path of forgiveness, but I eventually did let go and let God. I felt myself breathe again, and my life began to open up to the goodness that awaited me.

As I look back on my childhood as an adult, I now view that long ride from everything I knew to my final foster home as the deliverance into my new life. I moved out of darkness and into the light. I am able to recognize that forgiveness was the key to my happiness. I continue to do the daily inner work necessary to continue the healing process. As I embrace and accept all the success that has become possible in my life, I have also learned to love and accept love. I have a wonderful husband and two beautiful girls who have lives that are free of fear and family secrets. I know that it all began with that one step of forgiveness that was the catalyst for creating my new life and legacy.

I can attest that when you make the decision to forgive and let go, your life changes for the better. This is not to say that there will not be other hurdles you have to overcome in your life. I can tell you, however, that when they arrive you will be better equipped to handle them when you do the work to leave your past pains behind you and approach hurdles with a positive attitude.

You must no longer be willing to be held captive by those who victimize you, or to hold on to your family secrets out of fear or family loyalty. The authenticity and transparency in which you live your life are destined to touch many lives. Know that your message may be the message to heal another. With this knowledge you are helping yourself and helping others move from pain to possibility.

Nisha Jackson is known as the "Breakthrough Catalyst." She is an author, speaker, coach, and mentor to women and youth who are ready to change their mindsets, break through their pain, and create possibility in their lives. She has helped hundreds of clients create financial independence by breaking through limiting mindsets and building successful businesses. To join Nisha's community or have her speak or train at your event, please contact her at www. FinanciallyBrilliantWomen.com.

Living My Love Story… with Me

Zemirah Jazwierska

THIS IS MY LOVE STORY AND I WANT to share it with you. Up until the last couple of years I spent a lot of time in my life chasing love. I tried and tried to turn my life into my love story, but time and again I felt like I came up short. While I had a hunch that I wouldn't find love outside myself, I truly didn't know how to find it inside myself either.

For years I would go to the library and come home with stacks of self-help books. I read over and over that loving me was the answer to my search for love. The problem was I had zero clues as to *how* to go about doing that. I did the usual things: taped messages to my mirror, practiced nice self-talk, took warm baths on occasion, but nothing seemed to stick. Those nasty inner voices of "not enough" continued to banter back and forth in my mind, stealing any shred of love I was ever so briefly and temporarily able to encounter.

What I am about to share is how I ultimately found love and made it stay in my life. How I began and continue to create and live my own love story, day by day. How I eventually learned to be present with myself, making my life experience one giant epic tale of love. It is my hope that as a result of reading the words here on these pages, you are able to awaken your love story in your life. Maybe as you read this you will question and possibly find out what love really means to you. Maybe you will activate the power to meet life with a sense of acceptance. Maybe, even if just for a tiny bit, you will lose yourself in the moment and find peace.

Whatever magic is in store for you, I invite you to just hit the pause button on your life as you fall into these words. Allow yourself to simply *be*. Give yourself permission for the entire world to be okay, even if just for the time it takes you to read this chapter. I believe all great love stories begin with accepting ourselves and allowing all to be okay in our own minds, even if just for a moment.

The Ending and the Beginning

I was shot in the leg even though he aimed for my heart. I was shot for standing with integrity behind my truth in present time. I was shot because I could not love him. He had given me one last chance as he pressed the gun firmly against my chest, one last chance to say *the words*, to profess my love. I leaned into the barrel of the gun, my throat constricted. I could not breathe. But for once I was not paralyzed by fear, but rather silenced by my own integrity. I would no longer speak what I did not feel — words that were not authentically mine. In my present silence, as I leaned into the pain, my inner strength grew like a bright light spreading and infiltrating every cell of my body. My heart began to pulse with an ancient rhythm and I felt my primal connection to me. I was ready to face death, if needed, to preserve my most authentic self.

The painful recognition that I was not going to speak registered in his eyes. I met his blazing rage, feeling the enormity of the gulf, the immense chasm ever widening between us. The pain of abandonment and loss and the fear of annihilation threatened to paralyze my reserve, but I stood strong. I met his eyes, feeling a deep sadness, both our dreams instantaneously withering on the vine of the moment. Tears began to run down my cheeks as I allowed our pain to mingle intimately for the last time. We had done our best. We had loved each other the best we knew how; it just wasn't enough. It wasn't true love. It was... over. I could not truly love him because I could not truly love me. With a shout of rage he pulled the trigger, and the bullet, surprisingly, blasted through my leg. I immediately woke up from this dream.

It was 4:55 in the morning when I energetically left my old life behind. With this dream, my marriage took the final shot. Although it took quite some time for it to officially end — for him to remarry, completely shut down co-parenting, and sever all communication with me — this dream was the beginning of the end. It brought the realization that I would no longer live unaligned with my heart even if I had to claw my way back to the joy of life from the bottom of a deep well of despair.

On some level I deeply knew that as in the dream I would walk out of my married life temporarily immobilized rather than fatally wounded. On the surface, however, I was terrified. I had never paid my own bills. I had never lived alone. I had two beautiful daughters who depended on me to be emotionally, spiritually, and physically aligned. My mind, awash with hows and what-ifs, spiraled mercilessly away from my heart into full-on, head-centered living. As a result, I would spend the next six years seeking Neverland.

Chasing Peters

To find relief from what felt like the unbearable situation of the disintegration of my marriage, I busied myself chasing what I call "Peters." I call them that because most of them were like Peter Pan: men who were fabulously fun, but who essentially were deeply wounded orphans who didn't want to grow up.

I began an online dating marathon. I thought if I could just find a stable, comforting relationship, I could quell the deep emptiness and lack of love inside me. I was miserable, and my mind was bashing me with "You should be... [this or that]." I was sad. I was lost. I was lonely. And most of all, I was terrified.

As the man-search continued, I began to wear myself out. I dated men such as the Hungarian mason, the Ashram hopper, the infamous IT lawyer, the spine doctor, the rock climber, the farmer, the meditation writer, the trash collector, the Marilyn Monroe lover, the entrepreneur, the app builder, and, seemingly to me, the actual Peter Pan with whom I tried to forge a relationship for over two years. It didn't work, as you can imagine. With my neediness at an all-time high, I was a magnet for men who were charming, seductive, elusive, withdrawn, obsessively introspective, judgmental, image-driven, adventurous, intense, defensive, emotionally unavailable, controlling, fantasy-ridden, angry, and fearful. In retrospect it all makes sense; those were the signals *I* was sending out, so those were the types of people I was attracting. They were mirroring me back to myself.

My trek through Neverland culminated in the Land Down Under. On a whim I joined one of my dates, Mr. Wall Street, in Sydney, Australia, for a convention he was attending. After a few short days this date reached a catastrophic end and we both went our different ways. There I was, halfway around the world, still chasing some dream of love instead of experiencing it. I sat down in a pool of self-rejection, reflecting. I realized how attached I had become to creating and enjoying "later" while sacrificing the present "now."

One Little Word

Sitting there in the middle of that botanical garden in Sydney, I found the meaning of love. At first my head was swimming with a torrent of thoughts: *"How could I have allowed the dating to get this out of hand? What sort of responsible single mom travels to Australia on a date? Am I really that desperate? What exactly am I searching for?"* With those thoughts, something inside me reached a critical mass. Through all that thinking a silence began to take over, spreading like a slow fog, quieting the thoughts it touched.

I continued to return to the garden for the next few days. I sat in the grass or on a bench. I captured the beauty with my metallic-red Nikon camera. Each flower petal was its own being. Each flower itself had an entire world inside it. The enormous Australian trees seemed to speak, sending out their ancient vibrations of wisdom. My senses were tuned in to the world in a whole new way. I began to *feel* nature, to *breathe* with it, to merge. The more I focused on beauty in silence, the more the thoughts inside me let go. Serenity reigned. The entire universe seemed to quiet. My focus became ultra-sharp, like the point of a pin. Even though the noisy world of a metropolitan city wrapped with holiday buzz swirled around me, and a Christmas concert with thousands of attendees blasted on the other side of the garden wall, I was at the bottom of an ocean of silence, simply there… with me.

It was then that I encountered my meaning of love. After all that searching, one little word reverberated in my mind. One little word summed up the experience that was happening to me in that moment. That little word was *okay*. You might have been expecting something a little more profound, but it was really that simple. Yet as I would find, it was so very difficult to apply. With that realization, my love story truly began.

Living in Love

From that point on, that little word became the basis, the root, the foundation for everything in my life. On the journey back to the States, I was vibrating, broadcasting a new light within me. And I was attracting attention in a different way. A Hollywood writer offered me a ride from the airport to my home which I readily accepted. He was impressed with my awakening in Australia and suggested that I find a way to share it. Joyfully I got busy looking for "okay" in every single moment, every single event, every single interaction, every single person or thing.

Ever so slightly my life began to shift. I noticed that when I focused on what was okay, I could not focus on what was not. Know what? My starving heart began to get fed, nourished by my attention to what was okay. Whenever I found myself beginning to feel a little undernourished – to feel hungry for something more or something other than what was on the life plate in front of me – I returned to the very basic search for okay. What I experienced was more and more "okayness" with life.

It wasn't that I liked everything that was going on. In fact the opposite was often true. A condo I owned burned down. The girls and I continued to scrape by on a teacher's salary with minimal support. But the difference was that I began to accept all that was going on with it. And although I did not like it, I focused more on what to do about it than on my self-hypnosis with what I thought was not okay. I became freer to make choices aligned with feeling good.

Pretty soon my life changed dramatically and started to match my thinking. My love story began to grow and expand. I found ways to add more okay to each moment and aspect of life. The more I rehearsed looking at what was okay, the more my relationship to myself transformed and I found true self-love. Before I knew it I was feeling good more of the time than I was feeling bad. I felt as if I were even vibrating with love.

This vibration began to infiltrate all areas of my life. It became the common thread weaving it all together. My relationships with my daughters bloomed. As I put more okay in, we relaxed and began to deeply enjoy each other. My finances expanded and we prospered. No longer focused on lack and what was not okay, my bank account and how I related to money began to expand and grow, naturally, matching my belief system that all was okay. And I dropped the search for a partner and lived my love story solely with me.

Wouldn't you know it? A man intent on living his love story with himself soon appeared. We recognized each other as kindred spirits – a real match in many ways. Presently we are joyfully living our love story together and with each of ourselves individually.

Living Your Love Story

I invite you to try it out, to dive deeply into your own life and begin to build and strengthen your circuitry for love. Join me in putting more okay into every moment of your life. Here are three simple steps to get you started living your love story with you:

1. Take a few deep breaths and pull your attention back to you. Allow your awareness to separate from the story that is currently playing itself out in circumstances, almost like you are watching a movie on the screen that is life. Breathe as you detach from the story. This is how you bring your very best self possible to the moment at hand. Remember, your very best self changes from moment to moment, day to day. Allow that to be okay. You are just looking for the very best possible you for right now.

2. Now look for one little thing that is okay with you and focus on it. It might just be the simple fact that you are looking. Allow that to be enough. If you are thirsty, drink the very little drop that is in front of you. You quench your thirst by beginning to drink any drop that is available to you in the moment. See how much okay you can bring to the current situation. How can you add okay? Remember, this is not saying that you have to like it or that the situation is good or bad – this you do not ultimately know. You are just looking for any drop of okay that is available to you right now.

3. Decide what your options are. Think of as many as you can. Be creative and allow your imagination free reign. Even if the options seem highly unlikely, they are, in fact, options. Then feel into which one feels best to you right now, knowing that you can change your mind at any time. Ask yourself, for right now, which one feels the very best. Go with it.

A wise coach once told me, "Life is not about not falling down; it is about how quickly you get up." Falling down is an inevitable part of the journey. How quickly you get back up is up to you. Allowing yourself this freedom, treating yourself with acceptance, and nourishing yourself with understanding is the ultimate okayness.

Zemirah Jazwierska, Ed.S., works as a licensed school psychologist in Colorado where she has studied the impact of brain science and executive functioning on child development and learning. She is also a certified Neurosculpting Facilitator, empowerment coach, children's meditation facilitator, yoga practitioner, and author of the forthcoming book, *Finding Your Shangri-La: The Love Story within You*. Zemirah's life-long mission has been to spread enlightened ideas around the planet. Visit www. FindingYourShangri-La.com for more inspiration.

No Scar, No Wound?

NuLuv Jones

THE URGENT PLEA OF, *"No, Mommy, no!"* caused me to freeze. It was as if I had been jolted back to reality, yet time stood still. I looked over my left shoulder to find my two youngest sons' faces stricken with intense grief that matched the urgency in their voices. It was only then that I became acutely aware of the weight in my hands. I turned to see that the expression on my oldest (by a minute) son's face was identical to that of his brothers'. In that moment I recognized the gravity of the situation I had created.

To this day I still don't know how, or even why, I had picked up my first-born and was dangling him over the second-floor banister. Quite the mathematician, he was surely calculating the injury he would incur if I were to let go. My rational mommy brain (RMB) kicked in, deducing the damage my extreme behavior had already caused. It's a good thing RMB resides in the heart because ego had totally occupied my mind; it only had shame to offer. My heart genuinely wanted to know, *How did I get here?* I didn't have a clue, but as I struggled to pull my son back to safety I knew I had to find out. What I did know for sure was I couldn't afford another incident like that... or worse.

Shaking uncontrollably, I kneeled and wrapped my arms tightly around Darius as his brothers sighed in unison. My words nearly choked me as I looked into the eyes of my beautiful, brave seven-year old and attempted to apologize. Honestly, I couldn't form the words to adequately apologize for almost doing what I am convinced only God preempted. True to his nature of putting others first, he held me tighter and said, "It's okay, Mommy. I know you love me." Markell and EnRico were so relieved they nearly knocked us over when they rushed over to join us there on the floor. That day I promised Darius, his brothers, myself, and God that I would never return to that dark place.

I hadn't counted the price I would pay to keep that promise. As soon as I had a moment to myself I started to replay my life in my head. I quickly realized the events of the day were just another episode in the emotional unraveling that had begun to accelerate over a month prior. I didn't know how to make it stop. Until September 11th, 2001, I was convinced, *Tomorrow, I will be better. Tomorrow, I will begin again.* That was essentially the pep talk I had given myself since my last official day as a United States Army captain. But six months had passed and I still had not experienced any positive change.

Looking back on it, it was hard to admit, even to myself, that I had essentially come home, taken off my uniform, put on my pajamas, crawled into bed, and stayed there. Until 9/11 I had spent every possible moment of my day balled up in the fetal position in the center of my bed. It was my safe place. I dreaded time spent elsewhere. But I was a mom. I had to take care of my babies. I have often heard, "It takes a village to raise a child." Well, I had three children, but there was not one village in sight! I was my sons' lifeline as they were mine. My responsibilities of caring for my children were usually the only thing that forced me out of bed.

Despite my despair, I wanted them to have a sense of normalcy. It was just as important for me to hear my sons' laughter every day as I believed it was for them to laugh. In addition to caring for their immediate needs, I made an effort to make their bedtime stories fun as well as educational. When the fun failed to show up, I resorted to tickling sessions before tucking them in. Yes, laughter proved to be good medicine for us all.

A totally different scenario played out at night. After putting the guys to bed, I basically cleaned the house until I passed out from sheer exhaustion. I slept until I was awakened by thoughts I fought hard to suppress. The nightmares, kicking of covers, panic attacks, and cold sweats became more and more frequent as time passed. And I became more and more sleep deprived. Despite the fact that I spent most of my days in bed, my body still craved nighttime sleep. But I had come to accept that it was impossible to return to sleep once awakened. I would sometimes sit up so fast I'd grow dizzy. In any event, my first order of business was to look in on my sons. Fortunately they were sound sleepers, so I usually found them in blissful slumber. Then I'd check the alarm panel and the door and window locks, just in case. I spent the rest of the night pacing about the house. Irrational or not, I believed every little sound warranted closer investigation.

Though I'd already spent six months in bed, I was sure I was okay. I kept telling myself I just needed one more day of rest.

On September 11th, 2001, I turned on the television as I would sometimes do after getting my sons off to school. I wanted to see what was going on in the world beyond my front door. As crazy as it sounds now, television had become my means of staying connected with the outside world. I found the horrible scene of the 9/11 tragedy playing out on every channel I tuned in to. I had totally missed the "Breaking News" crawl at the bottom of the screen. I admit that it took me a moment and a few channel changes to realize I wasn't watching some over-the-top scenes from an action flick. I became paralyzed and my eyes remained fixed on the television. The "I'm okay" facade I had mastered over the years completely disintegrated at the sight of the planes crashing into the towers and the ruin they caused. The planes crashing into the Twin Towers, causing them to crumble, CRACKED ME WIDE OPEN!

As if on cue, the recording of my own traumatic plane experience began to play in my head. Though it had happened more than ten years earlier, I found myself back in that moment. I remember looking out of the window of the small plane as we sailed through the air. No longer flying, we were just gliding through the puffy white clouds over seemingly gentle waters below. The sky was a beautiful blue. What could go wrong in such perfect conditions? I watched as the plane started descending towards the center of the lake. Moments earlier I'd overheard the passenger sitting closest to the pilot ask him why there was a red light lit on the control panel. He had dismissed it, assuring her everything was fine. Just when I had begun to relax again, she nudged me and said, "I think something's really wrong with this plane." I didn't hear her, but the look on her face indicated she wasn't delivering good news. Confirmation of this came from the pilot when he yelled, "Brace yourself; we're going down!" Then he frantically shouted, *"Mayday, mayday!"* into the radio. What a surreal moment! I immediately looked at my friend who'd invited me on the trip and said, "This can't be happening. This kind of thing only happens on television." It was supposed to be a little fun trip before my inevitable deployment to war. The initial impact of the plane into the water interrupted that thought, proving just how real it was.

I relived that life-altering experience one grueling second at a time while standing there in the center of the room in my PJs. Remote in hand, eyes transfixed on the television, I started to feel very alone but completely exposed. That particular day I allowed myself to feel fully just how that prior experience had impacted my life, every facet of my being. Yes, September 22nd, 1990, was a major point of derailment in my life that I had refused to acknowledge, and September 11th, 2001, was its day of reckoning. Sure, I'd seen signs of the emotional trauma that I'd chosen to ignore, just like the doctors had each time they'd examined me. But they had only assessed the physical trauma I had sustained. They rambled on and on about my head, neck, back, rotator cuff, knee, ankle, and pelvic injuries. They even said I had suffered a heart contusion. But there was no reference to possible emotional trauma.

The airborne paratrooper in me refused to be sidelined, so when duty called, I responded. This time duty was calling in the form of a deployment to desert sands in support of Desert Storm. It was merely a couple of months after the crash. Though I was finally off of the crutches, I still had a noticeable limp. To make the experience more challenging, I was placed in charge of an aircraft of 250 soldiers. Having so much responsibility didn't afford me the luxury of inventorying my own feelings about the quandary I was in. Newly promoted 1LT Jones was off to war!

Witnessing the events of 9/11 caused everything I had felt, feared even, but refused to acknowledge to surface, and it was taunting me. I tried to distract myself by giving attention to the victims of the egregious acts replaying over and over on my television. My heart wept for their families. Then there was the likelihood of another war. I felt genuine heartache for the soldiers who would inevitably be deployed to support it and their families. However, my immediate concern was how to stop my emotional hemorrhaging. I completely lost track of time, but I must have spent hours trying to make sense of all the thoughts swirling about in my head. There was no denying my life had imploded, and I simply was not equipped to put it back together.

Recognizing this, I called the Veterans Affairs Medical Center (VAMC) to schedule an appointment to see a mental health professional. I had to talk with someone about my recurring nightmares, insomnia, reclusion, and all my other emotional chaos. When I finally got someone on the line, I was informed the first available appointment was a month out. Not convinced I could hold on that long, I mumbled, "I'll take it."

The incident with my son Darius occurred one day before my appointment. I knew I couldn't wait another day. Upon arriving at the VA Medical Center I marched right up to the receptionist. She demanded, "Last name and last four." After putting my information into the computer, she looked at me with a little smirk on her face. She seemed all too happy to tell me, "Your appointment isn't until tomorrow, Ma'am." I looked at the woman and calmly said, "You don't understand. My today is my tomorrow." But inside my head I'd snatched her by the collar, pulled her close to me, and yelled in her right ear, *"NOW! **RIGHT NOW IS ALL I HAVE!**"*

I have always believed that a little insistence pays. That day was no different. I asked and God answered. Or it simply could have been that the receptionist bought the *don't-push-me-'cause-I'm-close-to-the-edge* look in my eyes. In any case I was able to see a therapist. I spent an hour with her, peeling the scabs off my emotional scars. I felt better after relieving some of the pressure that had threatened to completely blow the lid off of my life. I returned home armed with two diagnoses: post-traumatic stress disorder (PTSD) and postpartum depression. I also had two prescriptions, one to put me to sleep and the other to wake me up.

This experience taught me that contrary to popular opinion, what you don't know *can* hurt you... and your loved ones. I was reminded of this fact many years after receiving my diagnoses. I was an extra in Tyler Perry's movie *For Colored Girls*. I was only on set for the scene I was in, so I didn't know how the story unfolded. I went to the theater excited about the possibility of seeing myself on the big screen. I had no idea I would be more profoundly moved by a part I wasn't even in than by my own, in which Michael Ealey depicted a tormented war veteran. The man dropped his two young children from the window of a high rise as their mom struggled to save them. My heart ached for the babies, their mother, and the emotionally wounded veteran. Yes, even the veteran! It is a societal misconception far too many people, maybe even you, are conditioned to believe that no visible scars mean no wounds. The character depicted in that movie was hurting in ways I identified with. I had been there and *almost* done that!

I thank God I sought help when I did! I did my research so I knew there was no easy fix. I did everything in my power to prepare for the long and challenging journey back to wholeness. I read everything I could find on both PTSD and postpartum depression. I joined support groups at the VA Medical Center and Vet Center, and in my community. I followed my doctors' orders to the letter, at least in the beginning. Then I developed the awareness and courage to explore other alternatives to find what really worked best for me. Fortunately I always maintained the counsel and support of amazing healthcare professionals. My journey of healing was not linear. Some days I took one step forward and two steps back. That was okay. It was par for the course. The important thing for me was to maintain hope and continue doing my work.

I am in a much better place today because I became my own best advocate, extremely vigilant in regard to my healthcare. In doing so, I replaced the darkness I once lived in with light. I work hard to keep my light burning in hopes of helping others see it is possible to improve their own lives. I have also learned to love myself, really love *me* and trust myself completely. I can now enter situations totally out of my comfort zone because I trust *me*. But more than my own self, I trust God. He loves me more than I have ever felt worthy of. In all that I have gone through, He has never left me and I know He never will.

What I know for sure is that when it comes to healing the heart, mind, and soul, the 180-degree turn you must make to reach wholeness is not an arc on the circumference of the pain. You must make an intentional U-turn right where you are – revisit the pain but not reside in it to get back to the other side. Healing and wholeness is yours for the taking. But *you* must do *your* work and go through the healing to get to the wholeness. Yes, go through it to get to it! You're worth it!

The Transformational Love Messenger **NuLuv Jones** is a Certified Life Coach and a Certified Parenting Coach. She is a former Airborne Army Captain, war veteran, and plane crash survivor who now assists others in overcoming challenges and navigating the pathway to their life's purpose. Her personal journey of coping with PTSD and postpartum depression while raising triplets alone fuels her passion to serve others. For more information on how NuLuv can assist you, please visit www.TransformationalLoveMessenger.com.

Inner Power Parenting

Tiffany Kane

May 9th, 2010

IT IS MOTHER'S DAY, ONLY THE THIRD one after giving birth to my son. In my head I am screaming over and over again, "No! No! No! This can't be happening! This isn't real! No! No! No!"

But all that escapes my lips is a shaky whisper: "I can't do this."

My father-in-law is standing behind me to my right with his left hand gently resting between my shoulder blades. He whispers back, "Yes, you can."

I am standing in the hallway outside the waiting room for family members of surgical patients. There is what feels like an army of faceless people wearing white coats approaching me. The one in front reaches out to grab my hand and says, "I am sorry, Mrs. Kane. Your husband didn't make it. We never started the surgery. He had a heart attack before we could administer any anesthesia."

Now, almost four years later, that is one of the few moments I remember of that day. I also remember sitting on the couch at my parents' house eating a sandwich. Other than that it is mostly a blur.

It wasn't that way during the months following that day. I used to replay every moment of every day of the week leading up to that event over and over in my head, wondering what, if anything, I could or should have done differently. Time has a way of helping me forget the unimportant details.

February 23rd, 2010
(two and a half months earlier)

My twelve-year-old nephew is ill. He is coughing a lot and his knee is bothering him. The doctor takes some blood to run a few tests and prescribes penicillin. My nephew breaks out in a rash. I am allergic to penicillin and discovered it when I had a similar rash. That must be what it is. My brother calls to let me know that the results from the blood work indicate that a trip to the children's hospital is required. When my husband and I arrive at the hospital, we are greeted with the news that my nephew is not allergic to penicillin after all, rather he has cancer. The doctors are not sure what kind of cancer yet, but they know it is aggressive and plan to treat it aggressively.

March 4th, 2010

My mom had been to the dentist, who suggested that from the look of her gums she might be anemic and should consider seeing her regular doctor. All the routine treatments for anemia have failed. Now it is time to take a look inside her body to search for the cause. Results indicate that Mom has colon cancer. Further tests reveal it has already metastasized to her liver. When cancer has spread from one organ to another, it is considered stage four of the disease.

April 1st, 2010

My husband, son, stepson, and I are living about fifty miles from my family. With all that is happening with my nephew and Mom, we decide it is better for us to live closer to them, so we move.

The first week of May, 2010

My husband's back is really bothering him. This makes sense. We just moved, he has been on a rather long road trip recently, and has been spending a lot of time in the car commuting back and forth to our business near where we used to live.

May 8th, 2010

The pain in my husband's back is too overwhelming now. He finally decides to go to an urgent care facility and is immediately sent to the emergency room. It is quickly decided that he is to be admitted to the intensive care unit. Somehow he has contracted a nasty bacterial infection that has caused sepsis (blood poisoning). All this time the pain in his back has been caused by his kidneys, which have been failing. His condition is serious. All through the night it is touch and go. His blood pressure is very unstable and dangerously low. He is scheduled for surgery early the next morning to remove part of his leg where it appears the infection entered his body.

September 22nd, 2010
(five and a half months later)

It is late at night, almost eleven o'clock. So far, with the exception of January, every month of this year has brought me huge, emotionally tough stuff to handle. Looks like September will not be an exception. My nephew, who had been diagnosed with cancer one day short of seven months ago, has just passed away.

My mom holds on for another year and a half. I am not sure if it is the cancer or the treatment that ends her life the year she would have turned seventy, on February 15th, 2012.

I had a plan for my life… and this was not it.

The last time I realized my life was not going according to plan, I engaged in some personal development work. My sole focus was to figure out why, in my early thirties, men were still complete mysteries to me. I wanted to get married and have a family, and I just couldn't figure out how to make that happen on my own. For nearly a decade I participated in weekend transformational experiences, went to seminars, and joined small weekly group meetings to deepen my understanding of the new things I was learning about how to create a successful intimate relationship.

Happily it worked. After a lot of reflective, deep, inner work, I became the woman who attracted the kind of man I wanted to marry. I met and married a man I loved deeply, and who loved me, too. Unhappily, he passed away four years and twenty-two days later.

Again I found myself thinking, "This was not my plan! I didn't do all that work to be a suddenly single mother of a two-year-old." My "plan" included a mom and a dad for my son. My "plan" included having someone to talk to when the tough stuff came up. And now I was going to have to do it all on my own. There were (and still are) many wonderful people in my life, but when it came down to it I wanted my husband and my mommy to help me navigate all of this unfamiliar emotional terrain. Neither one was available.

It is difficult to describe the depth of the fear and paralyzing self-doubt that consumed me when it came to thinking about raising my son alone. I had so many questions. I was rarely sleeping through the night anymore, and the hardest-hitting questions always seemed to come at three o'clock in the morning. The recurring theme of all I was asking myself was whether I was enough. Did I really have within me what it takes to raise a human being who will make a positive contribution in the world?

Looking in from the outside, people would be surprised to know I was struggling with the question of being enough. On paper I was completely prepared for parenthood. Before my son was born I had spent nearly twenty years working with other people's children in many different educational capacities. I was nearly finished with a doctoral degree in educational psychology, which translates to understanding human motivation and learning, and I had intensely studied child development. Bottom line, I appeared to have all the experience and book knowledge necessary to parent well. Besides, people have been doing this parenting thing for thousands upon thousands of years – isn't parenting something that should come naturally? Aren't we instinctually hard-wired to know what to do?

I discovered that just as knowledge and experience with other people's losses can't adequately prepare you for the death of your spouse, a child you are close to, or a parent, knowledge and experience with other people's children can't adequately prepare you for parenthood.

In a very short time my world had crumbled. Now that I had a son, I no longer had the luxury of time to attend seminars and participate in transformational weekends as easily as I could when I was single and only responsible for myself. So I turned to books. I read all kinds of them, but found myself continually reaching for and wanting to read more about spirituality. What started as a way to escape the pain and grief became a way of life for me. I continued to read and later added journal writing to my daily routine.

I noticed some interesting shifts beginning to happen. The fear and paralyzing self-doubt began to subside. Teachable moments with my son became obvious, and I found that I had the capacity to answer his questions with an ease and grace I had not previously known to be possible.

Making Personal Development Work for Parents

There are three key components to keep in mind as you embark on this great adventure of self-discovery:

1. **Figure out what works for you.**

   Successful self-discovery is a process that requires consistent practice. Your methods and mine do not have to be the same, but for me the process of personal development is highly dependent on reading, writing, good conversation with like-minded people, and spending as much time as possible surrounded by nature. For you it might be about physical activity, meditation, or a long motorcycle ride on a back-country road. The first thing to figure out is how to disconnect from the busy-ness of your thoughts and the world around you and discover the way within to the deep, inner knowing that wants what is best for you.

2. **Do NOT begin with the end in mind.**

   Personal development is a life-long process achieved through daily practice. There is no end, so do not look for one. Once you begin on this path the landscape will change and you will shift in unexpected ways, but the process will never end. Do not be intimidated by the idea that you *have* to do something significant daily, though. You can start with as little as ten minutes a day.

3. To get or to give? That is the question!

As you have read, I have approached personal development from two points of view. The first time I went on this adventure it was because I wanted to *get* married. The second adventure began because I wanted to make sure I had everything in my power to *give* to my son. Engaging in the process of personal development with an eye toward *giving* rather than *getting* is not only deeply satisfying, it is profoundly more powerful.

I believe that as a parent your decision to invest in your own personal development is the best gift you can give your child. On behalf of your child and the next generation, I honor you, I admire you, and I thank you for that gift.

Tiffany works with parents who desperately want to love the most important job they will ever have – parenting, but are overwhelmed by this major responsibility. Through coaching and seminars, parents learn to embrace the perfect parent within, eliminate self-doubt, and trust themselves. Tiffany is fiercely committed to empowering parents to raise empowered children who think creatively, communicate effectively, and take responsibility for their thoughts, words, and actions. Download your free MP3 audio program, *Raising Empowered Children,* at www.ConnectedToYourCore.com.

More Questions Than Answers

David Kloser

"YOU'VE GOT TO TAKE AN EARLIER FLIGHT! I'm changing it to tomorrow! I'm getting online right now to book you on the earliest one out in the morning. You can't go back this coming weekend. You've got to go now! I have a feeling your mom's not going to make it past this weekend!"

"Okay."

"Good. The earliest flight to Sacramento leaves tomorrow at six a.m. I'll call for a taxi to pick you up at four in the morning. Go upstairs and pack. I'll take care of everything else here."

"Okay."

"You might want to pack a suit… just in case."

"Okay."

The flight that I had booked a few months prior to fly out to visit my mom was suddenly thrown out the window. I had to get home to Sacramento from Baltimore as soon as possible, as my wife Christine "felt" that it was imperative that I be there.

Mom died around 12:45am on November 5th, 2009, of what they called "non-smokers" lung cancer.

* * *

I remember when I got the call. My dad left a message on August 20th. We were just finishing cleaning up after dinner and I couldn't get to the phone in time. I thought it odd to get a call from them that early in the day (Sacramento time). When I called back, my dad had an unusual tone to his voice. I knew something was up. He pretty much came right out and said, "Mom's got a spot on her lung and they said it's cancer." I asked what kind. He said, "Lung cancer, stage four lung cancer. She's going in for chemo tomorrow and for two treatments over the next six weeks, and they will re-evaluate."

"What is stage four lung cancer?" I asked. "And how bad is it? Does it go up to stage ten or something?"

"Stage four is the last stage. There are no other stages after that one," he replied.

Wow! The first thing I thought was, "But Mom is healthy! They were just out here in July on their way back home from taking a cruise. They are the most active people in their mid-seventies I've ever seen. How could this be happening?"

The ultimate prognosis wasn't good. The doctors gave her four to six months to live. We were hoping she would make it to Christmas.

* * *

That evening when I was packing, a peacefulness and calmness settled over me that I had never felt before. My movements were slow and deliberate. I felt like I was conscious of everything, as if I were learning something new for the first time. A sense of tranquility ran throughout my body and emotions. I was okay.

I sat at the edge of the bed to take a moment to reflect on what I was feeling. As I sat there, I sent my mom love, light, and peace, and permission to go. If she needed to be in a better place, she could go. She didn't need to wait to say goodbye to me in person.

My mom finally fell asleep in my parents' bedroom around 12:30am. My dad, brother, and sister collapsed in the kitchen to recount and reflect upon the five arduous hours they had just spent trying to get my mom calm and pain free.

Exhausted, the three of them decided to call it a night, too. My dad and sister went to check on my mom one last time before they went off to bed. They noticed that her chest wasn't moving. She had stopped breathing. She was gone... from this life at least. I wasn't there to speak to her one last time.

When I arrived at the Sacramento airport, my brother and sister were there to pick me up at the curb outside the arrivals section at the airport. They told me the news about Mom's passing before I even got my luggage in the trunk. They told me of the struggle they all had gone through trying to find comfort for my mom. They reassured me that it was probably best I hadn't been there. Forty-eight years of age and I'm still considered the baby of the family.

When I got to the house where I grew up, I went into my parents' bedroom. I felt a bit of a fright come over me as I walked down the hall to their room. I had never experienced death before in someone so close to me. The fact that it was my mom was rather unsettling, and I didn't know what to expect. I rounded the corner and she was lying propped up in a hospice bed. She looked yellowish and her face was a bit hollow from her weight loss.

One of the first things I noticed, though, was that she had the most peaceful, content look about her, and a slight little smile on her face. I stroked her hair and her arm. I saw that her right hand was clenched – to me representing the pain, struggle, and final departure from the physical world – and her left hand, her wedding ring shining brightly against her skin, was open and free.

The transition signs of her hands and the last expression on her face let me know she had found peace, unconditional love, and was welcomed home.

I spent some time in the room alone with her and had a little talk with her physical body. But something that I can't fully explain to this day was the remarkable connection I felt I had with her spirit; it was an essence of truth between us. I felt a sense of joy and happiness for her and for me, as well as a spiritual connection. I shared this experience with Christine when I saw her. She said, "Perhaps it was the connection with your mom that you've always wanted to have."

About an hour later, I believe, they came to take her away to be cremated.

There is a period between the death of a loved one and the actual funeral when the word has spread and friends begin bringing food to the house and sharing their condolences. I remember it was dark outside and a lot of my immediate family were hanging out in our living room – some sitting in chairs, some on the floor, almost like we used to do on Christmas mornings – recounting stories about Mom, Grandma, mother-in-law, in preparation for her eulogy.

"Here comes somebody else bringing us another dish of food," I thought as the front door gently swung open, temporarily stopping our conversation. Whatever they were bringing must have been heavy or involved a lot of dishes, because there was a delay when they must have set the food down, pushed the door open, and then bent down to pick up the food to come into the house. We waited for someone to enter, but no one did... physically. After a beat I said, "Oh, it's Mom!" My dad went over, closed the door, and said, "Hi, Dear. Come on in. We've been talking about you!" And then we all went back to chatting and sharing our favorite "Mom memories" as if she had actually joined us. I glanced around our living room to see if there was any reaction from the others, and noticed with interest that there was an empty chair. "That's for her," I thought. I believe my mom was right there with us.

You might be wondering why I am sharing this story. I believe that we all have lessons to learn in this lifetime. So what are my lessons? What is the lesson(s) for me to learn from my mom's passing? What does this all mean? Great questions! Maybe I'm not supposed to know the "why" behind these questions, or at least not right now. I guess I have to trust that I'll get the answers at some point in time. Or is it all right in front of me and I'm just missing the signs?

I believe that she, like all of us, had her own lessons to learn from her path, choices, and journey in this lifetime. I firmly believe that my brother, sister, and dad were there until the end – and that I and my other brother were not – for a reason. I don't know the reason. Maybe it's the soul contracts we have with each other. Maybe it was my mom's last way to take care of her baby. And what happens after we've learned our lessons? I don't know. Are they God lessons? Spirit lessons? Life lessons? I'm scratching my head as I'm writing this.

Did I pray for my mom? I think so. I know I sent her love, light, and peace, and hoped that she would make a smooth transition to the next realm, whatever that might be. But do we only pull out the "prayer card" when we're desperate for help? Is praying to God something outside ourselves? That He'll miraculously "fix" whatever's wrong? He'll make it all better for us? But maybe having something "fixed" is not for the highest good. I don't know. Seems at times I have more questions than answers!

The whole idea of spirit or God has been rather perplexing to me. I keep searching for the true meaning of the "what else is out there because it's bigger than life" thing. It's been a challenge for me to undo my interpretation that God is some old man with a white beard sitting in the clouds judging, granting wishes, and denying others access to heaven according to His whim. I don't understand it, but then again, am I supposed to? Perhaps not.

I've been trying to find my own connection to God. I have this certain expectation that I'll have some epiphany or great awakening, or get hit by a lightning bolt (in a good way) and see the light and be one with God! So my mom passes away and... and... and? Nothing! Yeah, some unusual things happened, but no lightning bolt. Like I said, it's an expectation of my own creation. And keep in mind that I didn't say it was a realistic one!

So I've been searching and studying about spirit (or that "something big out there") and doing what I can to make a spiritual connection with someone or something that is greater than me. Often I'm fearful of getting too deep in the discovery process, because who knows what I'll find? Frankly, this exploration is harder than I thought. Self-discovery on the spiritual path brings up a lot of stuff that is tough, and quite frankly I'd rather not face it! Perhaps it's easier to go through life dumb and happy, but I know that for me that's not the way to go. It's tempting. But as hard as this spiritual path is, and as resistant as I get, I know dumb and happy isn't right for me or my truth. Yet there's a part of me that feels my motivation for this spiritual enlightenment is fear-based. Part of me is drawn to the "All That Is," and quite honestly part of me is fearful of a hell.

It is intriguing to me as well. I've been meeting weekly with a group for a couple of years now studying *A Course in Miracles* by Helen Schucman and William Thetford, and reading the *Michael Handbook* by Jose Stevens and Simon Warwick-Smith and *The Power of Now: A Guide to Spiritual Enlightenment* by Eckhart Tolle. I get that we are all one, that God is within each of us, and that we are all spiritual beings having a human experience. But I don't feel it. What does my connection to God actually feel like? How can I feel that on a daily basis? These are the bigger questions I still have to answer.

It's been about four-and-a-half years since my mom passed. I think I've had only one dream in which I remember her, and I'm pretty good at remembering my dreams. I believe that I've dealt with the process of her leaving this physical earth. I didn't grieve, but had an amazing connection with her spirit, and I have moved on. But maybe there is more to discover!

What I know is that when I saw my mom for the last time, I really got that we are all just spirits contained in human bodysuits. I truly believe that it is up to each of us to form our own connections to God, the meaning of life, and how we deal with the big life questions.

I know that someday I'll find the answers I'm seeking, and wherever your path takes you, I hope you do as well.

David Kloser is a Certified Mental Game Coach and speaker whose passion is teaching life skills learned through baseball and developing the right mindset for success on and off the field. He's the author of *Stepping Up to the Plate,* for which he personally interviewed over 300 current and former Major League Baseball players, coaches, and Hall of Famers about handling adversity and achieving success at the highest level. David can be reached at David@SteppingUpToThePlate.com.

The Transformative Power of Love

Charlotte Lawrence

"Love is what we were born with. Fear is what we have learned here. The spiritual journey is the relinquishment – or unlearning – of fear and the acceptance of love back into our hearts...To be consciously aware of it, to experience love in ourselves and others is the meaning of life."
~ Marianne Williamson, A Return to Love

LOVE REQUIRES AN OPEN HEART. My heart was closed for most of my life until the day my son was born in January of 1988. I was thirty-three years old, and up to that point I hadn't experienced love and didn't know what real love felt like.

The day I gave birth, looked into the eyes of my child, and held his little body next to mine, I knew what real love felt like for the first time. When he was born, a deeper part of me that I hadn't been aware of awakened.

This started me on the long journey to discover the deeper meaning of life, open my heart, and experience love in the largest sense of the word. For more than twenty-five years that has been the focus of my life.

The Beginning of Fear

You might be wondering how a thirty-three-year-old woman having a baby had never experienced love. I'm sure you can guess that it's a long story of an unhappy childhood and a dysfunctional family, and you would be right.

I was a very sad and lonely child in a large family. I was the fifth of seven children, the youngest girl. My mother was an alcoholic, and died when I was twenty. I was emotionally and physically abused by my mother, and felt mostly ignored by my father, who died when I was twenty-nine.

It was a very chaotic home life. I grew up in fear most of the time. I was always afraid of what was going to happen next. Life was very scary and confusing to me. My mother could be very loving one moment and back-hand me the next. She was sick, I know that now. She was depressed and unhappy. As a child, there is no way to deal with all that craziness except to hide and try to survive.

Looking back now, I think my mother did the best she could. I really do. She was an excellent cook and made our birthdays and holidays special, but she couldn't maintain the effort and she would drink. With so many kids, I think her life became too much for her to handle. My father couldn't handle it either, and he dealt with her and us in his own way by escaping into his work. He was a good man, but emotionally unavailable. They were both frustrated artists and tried hard to dissuade me from being an artist, too. I wanted so badly to be loved and accepted for who I was. I wanted to be supported and cared for. But I wasn't, and it hurt me, particularly in my emotional development.

Getting Out of the House

I married my high school sweetheart at age nineteen and was divorced by twenty-one. I spent the rest of my twenties trying to figure out what life was all about and looking for love outside myself.

I was lost. I wasn't sure who I was and what I was supposed to be doing with my life. I was alone and on my own without much help and support. I had to figure it out for myself. The good thing about growing up the way I had was that I became independent and self-sufficient. The bad thing was that I was disconnected from people and life; I didn't trust anyone. And worst of all, I was afraid to ask for help.

Fortunately I made it through my twenties without making too many stupid mistakes. I went to art school and college. I was painting and selling my art. I worked at several interesting jobs and dated a lot of men. I lived on my own and supported myself, but I was still sad and lonely. I felt empty and disconnected, and was living a life without meaning or purpose.

In my late twenties something happened that changed my life forever. I found and read two books by Dr. Wayne Dyer: *Your Erroneous Zones* and *Pulling Your Own Strings*. That began my foray into the world of self-help books. It was just what I needed at the time. I needed to know there was hope for me, that I was not alone, and that I *could* change and improve myself and my life. I read more and more books trying to understand myself and life in general, searching for guidance and inspiration and how to connect with something within me that could help me feel better. Books were my lifeline at the time.

Starting this journey of self-discovery was very difficult. It was painful to feel the feelings that I had buried for so long, coming face to face with my greatest fears and beliefs about myself and life. Many times I didn't even finish books I started because it hurt too much to experience my own emotions. But it was a beginning, a small turn in the tide, the first steps on a journey that would lead me to freedom from my past.

Finding Meaning

By my early thirties my dream of being an artist had morphed into a career in graphic design. It was fairly artistic work, combined a lot of my skills, and I was good at it. I needed financial security and a direction in my life, even if it meant putting aside other dreams and desires.

I was still trying to figure out life and find my way in the world. My life looked okay on the outside. I was keeping it together pretty well. I had created a strong façade that I presented to the world, and had built a huge wall around my heart. No one knew how much I was suffering on the inside.

Then I met my second husband and thought I had found what I needed to be happy. I wanted a "real" life – to be loved and cared for – and maybe this was the way. Of course, I wasn't conscious of this at the time. It's become clearer in hindsight, after much soul searching and introspection. But I know now my heart was still closed to real love.

When I became pregnant a few years later, I was elated. For the first time I felt like a normal person living a normal life. I had a wonderful pregnancy, feeling connected to something larger than myself. When my son was born, my heart opened to love and I had real hope for a happier life. But I was still struggling with the pain of the past. I knew I had much more work to do. That's when I really started on my spiritual journey, but I had to fit it into my everyday life. That was the big challenge.

For the next twenty years I was a wife, mother, homemaker, artist, and employee, trying to hold everything together. I still didn't know fully who I was and what I was meant to be doing, but I knew there was more to life than I was experiencing. So the journey continued. I was still committed to my own personal growth and my dream of living with purpose. During this time I attended Al-Anon and Adult Children of Alcoholics. I tried different types of therapy, read hundreds of self-help books, took classes, attended seminars, journaled daily, started meditating, and, most important, found God.

After my son was born I had gone back to church after many years away from it. I felt a deep need to know God, discover my deeper self, and connect with my higher self. It was wonderful and painful at the same time. I found a new way of looking at life, of being in the world – a connection like I had never experienced. And I learned that I was still in deep denial about the emotional traumas of my childhood.

One day shortly after I had started attending church again, I was sitting there reading an affirmation, something like "I release and let go of any anger and resentment and open my heart to love." I remember thinking to myself, "I don't have any anger and resentment. Well, maybe a little anger, but definitely no resentment." Of course I was wrong. It took me many years to get in touch with the full force of my anger and resentment, and to really open my heart to love through acceptance of all the wounded parts of me and forgiveness of myself and others.

A New Beginning

My spiritual awakening and emotional healing accelerated after my son was grown, when my twenty-year marriage was coming to an end. It had been a long and winding road and I was starting to see the light and experience myself and life in new, more expansive ways.

By the end of 2008 I had experienced an epiphany of sorts. I realized that I had been living a dishonest life – a life that I *thought* I should be living, not a life that I had consciously chosen for myself. I had grown and changed. I knew I couldn't continue to live life as I had been. All the work I had done on myself – reading, healing, praying, meditating – had come to fruition. I knew I needed to make some big changes. I could no longer accept the life that I had so unconsciously created. For three years I wrote, prayed, and planned my next move, and, by the grace of God, made it happen.

In 2012, at age fifty-eight, twenty-five years after my heart first opened to love, I took the biggest and most purposeful risk of my life. I resigned from my long-term job, finalized my divorce, and moved back to my home state to create my life on my terms, doing what I'd been called to do – helping others open their hearts and create the lives of their dreams.

Life is good now. I love myself. I love my life. I'm blessed with loving family and friends, a supportive spiritual community, and a rich professional life. I'm living my truth and helping others live theirs. It isn't always easy. It's still challenging and an ongoing journey. But I'm awake and alive and I wouldn't have it any other way.

"Your task is not to seek for love, but merely to seek and find
all the barriers within yourself that you have built against it."
~ Rumi

Transforming Your Life

Looking at my life story, you can see that it *is* possible to transform your life by opening your heart to love and committing to your own personal growth and spiritual development. Through the transformative power of love you can heal the emotional wounds of the past and create your life anew.

The biggest step for me was connecting with the Divine Love of God. There are many ways to do this, and I suggest you find the path that's right for you. I did it first through reading self-help and spiritual books. Then I found a church that aligned with my beliefs about God and life. I learned affirmative prayer, practiced meditation, and participated in 12-step programs. I committed to the process and followed the path where I was led.

I now know that God is synonymous with love. When you're aligned with God you are living from love. You're more compassionate and accepting of yourself and others; more conscious and able to choose more clearly and creatively how to handle whatever issues arise in your life. You begin to take inspired action knowing that you're supported by life. For me, opening to Divine Love has been the ultimate blessing and the way to heal, move forward, and transform my life in every way.

Learning to love myself was another big step. For so long I didn't know it was possible. Early on I believed I was so flawed that I could never feel love. It took many years and a lot of work forgiving myself and releasing the past before I believed I was lovable.

To let go of the past and truly love yourself you must be willing to look at your life and fully experience the memories, feelings, and beliefs that arise. You can then forgive yourself or others, release the negative feelings, and surrender to love. Even though it may take time and can be painful, this practice will help you open your heart, feel compassion for yourself, and heal.

It's important to recognize that the real you is a spark of the Divine, not those negative thoughts and emotions. When you're able to truly surrender and align with the Divine Love of God within, you're able to love and accept yourself as you are. It's emotionally liberating. Loving yourself frees you from the pain of the past and makes it possible to create a new way of life in the future.

Love is needed in the world today. As you and I transform our lives, we're able to transform the lives of many others around us. As I have opened to love, I have created the possibility for others to do the same. That's why I'm here and that's why I'm sharing my story, with the hope that you're able to transform your life and help transform the world.

When **Charlotte Lawrence** answered the call to leave behind her thirty-year career as a graphic designer and do something more meaningful, everything changed. She now combines her design experience with her own personal transformation to help others open their hearts, live more fully, and design the life of their dreams. As a transformative life designer, Charlotte is a creative force in the field of personal growth and spiritual development. She can be reached through her website at www.CKLawrence.com.

Activate and Empower Your Inner Wise Self to Create Miracles in Your Life

SARK (aka Susan Ariel Rainbow Kennedy)

I THINK THAT MY WONDERFULL CAREER as a speaker and teacher really began when I was in the first grade. I came home and said to my mom, "Show and Tell should be me every day." She said, "Oh, Honey, the other kids need a chance," and I said, "No, they don't. They hate it. They're begging me to do it." Luckily I had a really neat mom who met with my teacher and came up with a plan for me to go to a different grade every day to do my version of Show and Tell. I always say that that's where I got my REAL speaker's training – when you're in first grade and have to hold the attention of sixth graders, you need to be reeealy good. I know now that what I call my Inner Wise Self was guiding me about how to speak to those kids and what to share. We all have an Inner Wise Self inside.

This same Inner Wise Self helped me write my first book when I was ten. It was called *Mice from Mars*. It was a very loosely disguised abuse story, which I'd experienced in my own family, and it helped me realize that my creative imagination could have a huge impact on how I lived my life. Writing that book was also my way of fulfilling a promise I'd made to be "a beacon of hope and write books for the world." When I shared this promise and dream with my family, my mom told me to eat my peanut butter sandwich. I kept going anyway.

I didn't create my next book until I was thirty-five years old. I procrastinated for twenty-five years because I felt afraid. Afraid I wasn't good enough, or didn't have the right to share my visions. Many, many lifetimes occurred for me during those years. When the day came to finally write that book, I wrote it in only two weeks. It's called *A Creative Companion,* and I created it in my Magic Cottage in San Francisco after I'd written a poster called "How to Be an Artist." It's my statement that we are all artists of life. I then learned that my Inner Wise Self had always been there and that I could activate and empower it to do even more. I began prolifically writing and creating as I'd always dreamed I would.

One of the main reasons I waited so long to write and publish my books was that I kept listening to my Inner Critics, letting them be in charge, and being disconnected from my Inner Wise Self. I want to show you how to connect with yours. When you can transform your Inner Critics and begin listening to your Inner Wise Self, you will discover you can be and do anything you imagine. Your Inner Wise Self is just waiting for you to activate and empower it to help you make all of your creative dreams REAL. Miracles will occur when you do this.

Everyone has Inner Critics. You can call them other names, but it doesn't really matter – we all have various forms of them inside us. Some of the most common Inner Critics are the Comparer, the Procrastinator, the Overachiever or Pusher, the Perfectionist, and the Hopeless. One of the really active Inner Critics for creative people is what I call the Comparer. The Comparer can get very frisky when we listen to authors or teachers speak and measure ourselves against them. The Comparer is especially active if you haven't yet put out your work in any physical form and it's still inside your head. You can actually stop yourself from doing what you love by using others to compare yourself against. I want to emphasize that you can, however, redirect that Comparer and have your Inner Wise Self be in charge with some transformational care practices.

Transforming the negativity of your Inner Critics is basically about the psychology of the self. The short version is that they developed when you were born and are still with you, and they're trying to protect you. They're not bad and they're not terrible; they're just there. They get scared. As you do new things, they can't relate. They're like, "Wait! Wait! That could lead to something bad happening!" I believe that everyone will benefit from having what I call an Inner Critic Care and Transformation System.

You can learn how to communicate with these parts of yourself and redirect them. First, identify that you have a part of you that's speaking inside your head that loves to give voice to everything it sees as negative. Then, once you identify that part, you can separate from the energy by saying "NO!" to that critical voice. I personally like to stand up and very loudly and powerfully yell the word "NO!" to my Inner Critic. Hearing my own true voice say "NO!" instantly transforms my energy and how I feel inside. You can try this right now if you're feeling any Inner Critics speaking inside of you.

Take a moment now to identify some of the things your Inner Critics often say to you. You might want to write them down on a piece of paper you can recycle later. Next, say "NO!" to those voices. You can do this energetically with your thoughts, but as I mentioned earlier, I highly recommend you stand up and say it as loud as you can. Perhaps you'll put your hands up in front of you as if to say "No! Stop!" with a hand gesture.

The next level of silencing the Inner Critics is reassigning them to other jobs. Critics need to work, and they don't care what they work on. If you don't redirect them, they will go to work in every aspect of your life. Let me give you an example. I have a very active inner Perfectionist, as many creative people do. I have given my Perfectionist an imaginary job. I say "imaginary" because I want to emphasize that this dialogue happens in your mind. You're going to invent a new job for your Perfectionist. Mine happens to work at an egg factory, checking for eggs that are cracked. This job was no longer big enough, so she's recently been promoted to supervisor of world egg factories. All the factories in the world that produce chicken eggs are being supervised by my inner Perfectionist.

It's a big job to handle, but my Perfectionist still comes sneaking back. She'll show up at the oddest moments, saying things like "Well, are you sure you're saying the right things? Maybe you're too loud. Maybe it won't work." It's my job to say to her, "No, Honey. Get back to the egg factory. There are lots of cracked eggs to look for and you need to leave me alone." I've even gone so far as to draw up contracts and agreements with my Inner Critics. As of the writing of this chapter, my Pusher and Overachiever are working at Miraval, which is a fantastic spa in Arizona. They are in charge of all the personal growth programs at Miraval because, you see, the Pusher and Achiever need something to really accomplish.

The third level of banishing those destructive Inner Critics is dialoguing and communicating with them, which I teach people to do with the help of their Inner Wise Selves. Think of your Inner Wise Self as being a giant coach or mentor that's already inside of you. Some people call it their higher self, pure positive energy, intuition, or Holy Spirit. I happen to call it the Inner Wise Self. Utilizing this part of you throughout your life means activating and empowering it so that it, and you, are in charge of your Inner Critics. Learning how to do this makes an unbelievable difference in your life. Most people know that they have an Inner Wise Self, but don't ask it for help in their lives on a daily basis. Most people are having inner dialogues with their Inner Critics.

While most of us would like to not have that negative dialogue running through our heads, we shouldn't be as concerned about *not* having it as we are about *transforming* it — caring and tending to it so it's no longer in charge of running our lives. The majority of people are being run by Inner Critics, resulting in a lot of crabby, unhappy, unfulfilled people. I'm glad to share the transformative tools that really work to change this.

One of the best ways to have a dialogue with your Inner Wise Self is to take out a sheet of paper and allow it to write you a little love note. Take a deep breath and ask the question, "Inner Wise Self, what do you have for me right now?" and write down what your inner voice tells you. Write down the words you hear even if they seem odd or strange to you. If you hear, "I know that you can be successful at whatever you do. You have the courage and power to be whatever you choose to be," listen to and make note of those love messages. They will help you silence and shift the Inner Critics more effectively than trying to simply ignore them in the hope they will fade away.

Once you've done this, sit down and take a few breaths. Close your eyes and once again tune in to your Inner Wise Self. Once you've written yourself a love note, from the perspective of your Inner Wise Self, just let all that wisdom sink in. Don't worry if it seems like you're making something up – your Inner Wise Self will show up to help you and share unconditional love with you. Then keep asking and dialoguing with your Inner Wise Self about everything – not just the big subjects, but about everything in your life. The more often you practice, the stronger and more activated this part of you will become.

Just so you know, I've experienced and transformed financial difficulties. I've had debt and transformed that, too. Business partners have left me, and I transformed my business as a result. I've transformed every kind of challenge and experienced every kind of joy, magnificent success, love, and all the other great things; and it's that strong connection with my Inner Wise Self that allows me to live a truly creative, magnificent, self-loving life.

Integrating this process into your personal and spiritual growth practice will truly transform your life. I share this truth from my own experience, knowing that if I hadn't done this for myself, and kept doing it, I never could have impacted the lives of millions of people around the world and lived so happily while doing so. The possibilities are infinite and they all exist within you – as you are right now, with no "improvements."

Let this moment be the time you turn down the volume on what your Inner Critics are saying and let your Inner Wise Self grow larger and be activated and empowered to be in charge of those Inner Critics. Allow your visions and dreams to become REAL. Be the human channel that brings them down to earth for us to see, experience, and enjoy.

SARK, also known as Susan Ariel Rainbow Kennedy, is a bestselling author, artist, and Succulent Wild Woman, with sixteen titles in print and well over two million books sold. Her purpose in life is to be a transformer, an uplifter, and a laser beam of love. She does this through her art, words, and spirit.

Synonymous with transformation, healing, movement, and FUN, above all things SARK has spent the last two decades serving women and men around the world, helping them activate their creativity and Inner Wise Selves, accept themselves more fully, and embrace laughter every day.

An acclaimed speaker and teacher, **SARK** is a transformational role model offering inspiration and guidance to people in their process of living more powerfully and authentically and being more actively creative on a daily basis. She lives and creates gladly in San Francisco with her beloved partner, John.

Healing Empty

Jacqueline Lawrence

I AVOID SCALES. I am not a fan of the story their numbers tell. Each pound carries a different fear. Each fear stacks itself on a different skeletal bone, a different organ. I feel the weight in each belabored breath, each belabored step I take. For years I've looked in the mirror and wondered, "How did I get here?" One day I stopped listening to my head and finally began to hear my body's unexpressed feelings.

Mirror, Mirror

Mirror, mirror
tell me, tell me,
how did we get here?
does my arm swallow
the sleeve of my shirt like yours?
does my sweater stretch
to cover my belly like yours?
do my legs rub together like yours?

Mirror, mirror
tell me, tell me
what are you hungry for?
what did you fear then?
what do you fear now?
where do you hurt?

Scarcity scares. Scarcity scars. It gets easy access when survival is a constant companion, playing and replaying the "not good enough" soundtrack in my head: I am not smart enough; I am not beautiful enough; I am not worthy enough to be loved. With scarcity, it is easy to fall between the cracks, and easier still to fill in the cracks with empty calories to numb feelings I do not know how to feel, or do not want to feel, so I can disappear.

Disappearing Act

I don't know when I stopped looking in mirrors.
I can't remember when I stopped taking pictures.

I used to love to play dress up with my mother's bangles and necklaces.
I used to mark milestones with pictures in the park, by the seaside,
In restaurants with friends celebrating birthdays, promotions.

I began to extend my lazy Sundays, lying between lavender sheets,
To Mondays and Wednesdays and Fridays and sunny days.

I don't know when the lavender scent faded.

It must have been around the time I began to carve out small and smaller spaces
to squeeze my two hundred and plenty frame;
to hide, to disappear...

To be invisible.

Scarcity screams silently. My fatness was my loudest voice at its highest blood-curdling pitch. It was my cry for help. Family and friends responded with sage advice. Some advised me to keep my weight down to prevent heart disease, diabetes, and high blood pressure. Others told me if I didn't like how I looked I should do something about it. As a former athlete, I knew something was blocking me from remembering and doing what I had done for years to condition my body to be at peak performance. As a result, in 2009 I declared I would excavate and release all that no longer served me and prevented me from fully living the life I desired. It took me another year to open cobwebbed Pandora's boxes, complete medical tests, and conduct research to decide on the best program to help me release one hundred pounds.

After putting together a group of friends as my health and well-being support group, I started a twenty-six-week medically supervised weight-loss program. At first I steadily lost one to three pounds per week. However, during week five, I lost seven pounds. Almost immediately I heard myself telling myself that I could not sustain or maintain this level of drastic weight loss. I stayed in my comfort zone and lost one to three pounds per week. At the end of the program, while I was disappointed I did not meet my goal, I saw my almost fifty-pound weight loss as a step in the right direction.

Three months after the program ended I slowly began to regain the weight. For the first time I did not beat myself up, because I had come face to face with how quickly I take myself out of contention to fulfill the deepest desires of my heart, and how quickly I separate myself from my true self. It was now clear to me that my weight was not only about my weight. I took this as an invitation to go deeper, to uproot the feelings, reasons, and excuses that subconsciously drive my hunger and my choices to hide, to be invisible.

Hunger

My question for her:
Did you want me?

My question for him:
Where have you been all my life?

She stayed...
To be both mother and father —
Willing to give her life, the clothes off her back.

He stayed away —
Not a phone call or dollar sent...
For school or life supplies.

I can count on one hand
the number of times
I heard her say — I love you.

I can count on one hand
the number of times
I saw him face to face.

I hungered for her affection...
I hungered for his attention.

Scarcity seeks submission to blame. Scarcity wanted me to end my journey there. However, when I stopped at blame, I was stuck in judgment and quick fixes for complexities I did not understand. I still do not know the experiences that influenced my mother's actions to not speak her feelings of love. But when I step into her shoes as an immigrant and a black, single mother, I feel her fear and her worry. And I still do not fully understand my father saying it wasn't his fault that he was absent from my life. But his answer freed me to unpack feelings of rejection and abandonment that I had felt for years. If I had stayed in blame, I would have missed that my parents love me the best way they know how. Their love is complete and more than enough. I now tell my mother I love her, and she has begun to say "I love you" to me more and more. And I now accept my father's "I love you" as his hug from a distance.

As I inched towards my weight-loss goal, I knew this new clearing was only the start. There was still something blocking me from accepting compliments and support from family and friends who were noticing my weight loss. If I had stayed in blame, I would have missed the abundance of their affection and attention for me. But even more important, I would not have continued my exploration to also discover that scarcity shames, scarcity silences, and scarcity walls secrets.

Hide & Seek

He came into the house. Invited.

Seven, eight and nine year old girls
ran around playing hide and go seek while
someone went somewhere for a quick minute.

A minute or less was all he needed
to back me into my hiding place.

Behind the door that separates the living room
from the dining room. His eyes held me in place. Quiet.

For 38 years, I stayed quiet.
For 38 years, knocked knees stayed cemented in ceramic tiles.

I remember breathing. His. Mine.

I remember the minutes that dropped between each breath.
I remember my belly turning and churning its juices.

I remember the seekers' flip flops clicking and squeaking
on just polished floors, as I waited...
waited for his next move;
waited for her to turn the corner;
waited to be
unfrozen.

It's scary to thaw out thirty-eight years of silence, thirty-eight years of shame, and thirty-eight years of unknown secrets. At the end of a meeting with my life coach, he asked me to reflect on when was the first time I experienced being vulnerable and attached. Later that night, a splintered image appeared in my dream. Slowly another image surfaced, and then another, like pieces of a puzzle. Faces and scenes from long ago began to take shape as a long-lost memory. I felt stuck again. I felt frozen again. I woke up in a cold sweat.

Over that weekend I came face to face with my nine-year-old shadow operating system (SOS). This was the turning point when I began to build a discriminatory reaction to light-skinned black men. I created a story that they were cocky because of their privileges since slavery days, yet they were the men who asked me out the most. I could not understand why the universe kept sending them my way. Now I know these kind, sweet, and loving beings were my guides to new depths of healing.

This was also the turning point when food became my refuge and fatness became my protector. This was the turning point when I began to play less (until grade seven when I rediscovered sports) and read more to lose myself in far, faraway places. This was the turning point when I began to isolate and insulate myself from boys and men. And this was the turning point when I began to internalize shame. In that moment, I chose to believe that no one would love me because I was fat. The truth is I never lacked attention from men. I have had men run after me while I was sitting on a train. I have had men pursue me to be their wife, their girlfriend, their baby mother, their lover, their friend. I did not trust their interest, their intention. And when a man reappeared in my life, tracking me down like I was a lost treasure, mirroring my fear, I knew it was time to choose a new belief.

With this experience I understood that the treasure that was lost was me. I thought for years I was hiding from others, only to discover I was hiding from myself. It was no longer about other people discovering me; it was me creating me. At first I was very uncomfortable with this lesson, and there are still days that I still am. Shedding old skin is a scary thing. Now it was time to risk being with all the things I feared people would use to judge me: my imperfections, my mistakes, and my disappointments. For the first time I chose me over others. This included dropping out of my relationships with family and friends for a three-year period. I lost some friends during this time. They thought I had abandoned them. I did not have the words then to let them know, and let me know, that if I did not separate from everyone's expectations of who and what I should, could, and must be, I would drown, lost to me forever.

Scarcity surrenders reluctantly now that my soul is satisfied. I now live in questions that connect, instead of separate, my spirit, mind, emotions, and body: What is my purpose? What does the Divine within want me to give today? I no longer feel the need to prove myself to anyone or to overprotect my heart. I no longer feel the need to please anyone at the expense of starving my soul. To ensure this was not only a revelation, the universe sent me back in time to grieve a relationship with a man whom I now know was in my life for a season to help me to discover that I am smart, I am beautiful, and I am worthy of being loved – just as I am.

A Muse

I thought I may amuse you —
Never be your muse.

Your words sculpt the fit of our hugs
by the sea, in the rain.

Your words contour beguiling depths
beyond the shallow end I used to play.

Your words color the landscape of my black and white
and grey thoughts, with sunrise and sunset hues of red and gold and orange.

Your words, your words spark fire in my Rubenesque ebony belly
awakening mouth-watering desires, melting seduction's sweetness.

Unveiling my amusement, my amazement,
As I savor and share the richness of my hunger.

In this relationship I got a glimpse of me when I showed up with curiosity, fully self-expressed and willing to see the gift and the beauty of perfection in our imperfections. I did not eat my regrets when this relationship was over. I was instead thankful for who I was becoming as I take the risk to be me.

This "healing empty" leg of my journey has left me with many lessons, two of which are:

1. Weight loss is not only a physical journey; it is also a spiritual, mental, and emotional journey.

   I learned that spiritually I was separated from my true self, and one of the results was that I entangled self-esteem and self-image. This contributed to my being mentally distracted with cluttered, incessant thoughts comparing myself to others. I feel emotionally lighter now that I know old wounds and hurts can heal the emptiness within to house and host love. And I physically reconnected with an energized body fueled, instead of medicated by, food, decreased pain, and increasing ease of movement, breath, and rest.

2. Enjoy each step and each leg of the journey.

I am not yet at my hundred-pound release destination. However I have learned that each phase has its own transformational gift to be appreciated and each phase is preparation for the next. Recently I ended my almost twenty-year self-imposed ban on looking at my body in daylight. I saw my pear-shaped body as a mountain – my Kilimanjaro. For the first time I saw, appreciated, and embraced the strength and vulnerability of my body. For the first time I was in awe of my body's beauty. I apologized to me. I forgave me. And I thanked my body for being my travel companion, my teacher on this journey called life. It was then that I chose to believe I could step up powerfully to live purposefully, joyfully, and peacefully.

My Kilimanjaro

Slow and steady
the climb to my Kilimanjaro.

When I saw black shadow dance with white light
I cried I am sorry:
Sorry for wanting, waiting, and worrying how others will love me.

When I saw grey light bounce off cocoa brown skin

I asked me to forgive me:
Forgive me for not knowing how to love me.

When I saw blue hue shimmer across breasts and thighs
I said thank you;
Thank you for crossing the saddle to give freedom's access code — love me.

In the last couple of months I have begun taking the battery of tests to ensure that all is well for me to embark on the next leg of my weight-loss journey.

I am ready to climb my Kilimanjaro.

A diversity strategist by day, poet by night, **Jacqueline Lawrence's** mission is to heal hearts through words. As a published poet and author, she enjoys the journey to dance with curiosity, vulnerability, and paradox to mine possibilities and sacred wisdom. She's very excited about her forthcoming book, *Invisible Visibility: On Being Black, Fat and a Woman.* Please visit www.JandLawrence.com to learn more about Jacqueline.

The Power of Love

Char Leonard

BEING A CHRISTIAN, I OFTEN SPOKE of the "angels rejoicing at births and deaths," but never gave them identities, much less certain responsibilities! Our two sons and I were privileged to be witnesses to and recipients of the Power of Love through my dying husband's account of his angelic greeting party. Was it possible our angels are more active and influential than I ever credited them for being? That day began my angelic maiden voyage and played a major role in the life of our older son.

My husband, David, was sick for a decade, knowing the light at the end of the tunnel was an oncoming train, and this took its toll on not just the patient but the family as well. Unbeknownst to him, my soul mate was the victim of zinc toxicity due to daily use of an over-the-counter product, and in 2001 he began to exhibit central nervous system degeneration. The first real sign he was in trouble was when he cut his toe with the weed-eater and didn't know it! The blood dripping onto the kitchen floor when he came in from the yard was just as much a puzzle to him as to me. That episode sparked a whirlwind ride on the medical merry-go-round to discover the culprit and stop the ravaging symptoms in his body. Although his feet and legs were numb, the nerves in these limbs felt like they were on fire, and pins-and-needles sensations were his companions 24/7; it was as if his brain no longer communicated with his feet, but his pain impulses were in high gear.

I say the above to set the stage for his demise: the experimental treatments, the infamous I-don't-know shoulder shrugs of the physicians, dependent mobility devices, altered vehicles and living quarters to accommodate the disabilities… and even through all this his spirit never faltered and the smile never changed! But not so much with me, his wife of forty-plus years and his primary caregiver, nor with his adult sons. I still remember images of our older son cradling his father like a child while carrying him to the restroom. (Time was of the essence and David could not get into the wheelchair and make it in time.) Times like these our son would scoff, "This is your God? Your loving God is torturing my father!" I would always respond with my truth: that I believe everything happens for a reason. And although I was not sure why David's journey was so tormenting, I believed it was purposeful. But our son did not until THAT day.

"What does this have to do with angels?" you might be wondering. And I'd respond, "Patience, Grasshopper!!"

On his last visit to the pain specialist for a refill of the synthetic snail venom in his intrathecal pain pump, we heard the dreaded words: the pump had twisted and sepsis had been noted by the doctor. (Sepsis is a whole-body inflammation caused by severe infection). We were told to take him home and make him comfortable. For four days infection ravaged his body, causing episodes of delirium. His organs began to shut down, and he was taken to the hospital for the last time. Having been told in 2005 that he had six months to live, David had long proven that his desire to live was stronger than his physical strength. Outliving the death prognosis by six years, his body weakened by the hour.

For the next three days David's condition continued to roller-coaster: Get a little better, get a lot worse. But as long as he had bouts of getting better we thought this was just another rally for him. The doctor came in and had "the talk" with both of us. (You know… the one *no one* wants to have or participate in.) Doc strongly suggested that David be transferred to a hospice facility, and even recommended a facility in South Austin. He suggested we meet with the hospice rep and make arrangements ASAP, so we followed his suggestion and met the rep in the hospital room. As tears streamed down my cheeks like a constantly-fed river, David's words set the tone for our *aha!* moments. You see, after being married for forty-two years, David did not want to leave me. He point blank told the hospice rep that if there wasn't a bed for me, he wasn't going! The hospice rep politely said we weren't ready for hospice and to call her when we were.

Three hours later David went into a coma and his body began to lose its battle to stay alive. Our sons and I sat in the hospital room watching his labored breathing, knowing we needed to accept the inevitable. But we still spoke of recovery and the future, for this had been the scene many times before. David was like a real-life Superman! But this time would be different.

For thirty-six hours he lay non-responsive, his body and spirit playing tug-o-war between Heaven and earth. Although his physical being showed signs of shutting down, he fought hard not to give in to this demon that destroyed his body. And now we knew why. The decision to move him to hospice was made. When the EMTs came to get David, our older son said to them, "If he wakes up, don't tell him he is going to hospice." I thought this was a sign of denial on our son's part, but little did I know it was a stepping-stone to be used in a grand way very shortly.

It took us about forty-five minutes to drop the wheelchair off at the house and get down to the hospice. Nervously we talked about what we suspected the next few days would entail. The walk through the front door and down the hall to David's room conjured an odd feeling in me – one of desperation for life, but at the same time of acceptance and peace for death. When we opened the door to David's room, we were given the best gift ever! After being in a coma for thirty-six hours, David was sitting up in his bed, eyes wide open, excitement on his face like a child on Christmas morning, and words flowed from his mouth with clarity and purpose!

"My mama came to get me," he said. "She's driving a light blue 1967 Chevelle Super Sport and she has Uncle Pete, Roy Vaughn, Buddy, and Aunt Ruth… but not Joe's Ruth. They left Buddy here! Doesn't he look good? They went to get gas and will be right back!"

There was no time for conversation as he immediately drifted back into a coma. For the next twenty-two hours we sat at his bedside and dissected the now famous "last words" and applied them appropriately.

- The car was no surprise. David and I met drag-racing. (He won the race and could have taken my car, but instead took my heart.)

- His mother driving and bringing the others was so very appropriate; she was an angel on earth and would never leave her children.

- Those in the car had all transitioned to a higher dimension, but the mention of Buddy looking good was pivotal. (Buddy had passed from head trauma, and our last viewing of him was anything but good.)

- His articulation of which Ruth was in the car – "not Joe's Ruth" – stems from the fact that two of his uncles, Bill and Joe, both married women named Ruth. You guessed it: Joe's Ruth had not passed at that time.

You see, there was a reason our older son had been inseparable from David during the end stages of David's life. By his being present, there was no room for doubt, no misunderstanding, and no need for clarification. His father's dying words were absolute and affirming of God's promise of life after death and the promise of health. Yes, there was pain associated with watching his father suffer the perils of being a pain-ridden paraplegic for nine years, but knowing in another realm that his dad would be pain free, walk again, and dunk basketballs like back in the day made the immediate loss bearable. Now, armed with the knowledge and proof of God's presence in this situation, our older son's faith was renewed and his spirit was at peace! He was so inspired by his father's last words that he gifted the book *Heaven Is For Real* (the account of a six-year-old boy's trip to Heaven and back) to those friends who had suffered the loss of a dear one. And with every copy he'd write the following inscription on the front page: "It's true! My dad told me!"

David's words had a profound impact on both of us, but the impact on me was different than that on our son. I now longed to know more about where these angels stay when you're not dying. Like… obviously they have fast cars, so what else could be going on around us? Thus began my angelic education and introduction to the angels God placed in my corner and the talents assigned to each of them.

On my search for answers I took healing and angel-card-reading classes, networked with other angelic presence believers, and learned how to use meditation to deepen my walk with God and open communications with my angels. Thus Mama Char, the "no foo-foo woo-woo," emerged, and through my healing sessions I have come to depend on my angels assigned to lead, guide, and direct me to a fruitful and rewarding life of healing. Having had a small glimpse of the possibilities through David's final words, I am so grateful God opened that window and gave me the strong curiosity to learn more.

I can't even begin to tell you how this has changed our lives, especially mine. God's gift has strengthened our belief that HE is in control and everything truly does happen for a reason. The Power of Love, in our case, is like an onion: layers upon layers, each one as tasty as the other.

In closing, I'd like to share with you the amazing words our sons wrote to be read at their father's memorial service. To me these eulogies are the epitome of the Power of Love!

Dad
By Tiger Leonard

As I sit here next to you,
Your last breath not far away.
I think back over my life,
The way you loved me each day.

You are truly my hero,
My Superman and even more.
The wind beneath my wings,
The man I will forever adore.

You were there when I needed a hug,
When I laughed, when I cried.
No matter what you had going on,
You were there for every sport I tried.

You were the dad my friends wanted.
The person I wanted to be.
You will live with me in my heart,
But now it's time for you to be free.

The pain you have lived with,
The suffering you have endured,
No person deserves that life,
A disease that can't be cured.

It's time for God to call you home,
My heart hurts and I am so sad.
But now it's time to say goodbye,
I love you more than life, Dad.

Dad
By Herb Leonard

I, like my mother and brother, am so grateful for the support and love provided to my family over the years.

I love and admire my father more than any phrase, word, or gesture could ever express. He has always been my Superman and I would be so proud to become just a fraction of the father he is to us. I say "is" simply because his teachings and love will always live on.

I cherish memories of walking behind him in the grocery store, looking at how powerful and majestic his presence was, him teaching me how to be the best shade tree mechanic, and how to fight.

Those are just among the many memories I have. I am blessed to have him in my life. Rest comfortably and among loved ones.
I love you, Dad.

Stay tuned… Mama Char has just gotten started!
   Blessings…

Mama Char is an inspirational author, speaker, and overall entertainer whose life passion is to incorporate the gift of healing laughter into all. Often referred to as the "Queen of Silver Linings," her winning personality of "Dear Abby collides with Joan Rivers" allows her to speak the truth with passion. To follow her quirky outlook on life and realign *your* life, please visit www.MamaChar.com.

Following a Dream Back Home

Dinah Lin, MBA

I WAS DOWN ON MY KNEES, forehead to the floor, hands clasped in prayer. I pleaded, "Please God, tell me what I should do next!" Panic, fear, despair, and desperation engulfed me!

For months I'd been hoping to turn around my growing losses in the stock market. This was 2000, and the "tech bubble" had burst. I could say I was one of the lucky ones; I did not have a house to mortgage and had not borrowed, but my trading forced me to liquidate both my retirement accounts, wiping out my life's savings.

How had this happened to me?

I had an MBA in finance, a successful career in the corporate world, and had prepared for my latest venture by taking classes in trading stocks and options. Ah, yes – I learned just enough to be dangerous to myself! I was buying and selling options with names like "naked calls," "naked puts," and "butterfly spreads." Thinking about it now I can only claim temporary insanity!

I began trading in 1998 after "retiring" from the corporate world. My objective was to make some extra money then follow my dream: go live in China, study Chinese, and reconnect with my roots. I had no idea what a slippery slope I was on as I became addicted to day-trading. Trading options eventually left me with just 10 percent of my life's savings, barely enough for twelve months of living expenses.

Beneath my feelings of panic and fear, I felt immense sadness and sorrow, failure and shame. I had let myself down. I had failed, big time! I was accustomed to success and winning, not failure and losing! Not since my divorce two decades earlier had I felt such pain and sense of failure.

There were lessons for me in this experience, and humility was a big one!

Going to Beijing!

I can see the moment so clearly. My mom and I were standing in her kitchen in the house she and my dad had built in Williamsburg, Virginia. I had meant to break the news to her gently, but I blurted out, "Mom, I've given this a lot of thought, and what I really want to do is to go to China to study Chinese."

Silence.

She looked at me. "Dinah, at your age? Forget about it!"

I was fifty-eight.

Knowing Mom, I knew she meant well. She pictured me moving halfway around the world to a place where I didn't know a soul. She knew how hard it would be to learn the language. And she knew my financial situation was precarious.

In the weeks leading to my decision, my left brain, stuck in survival mode, shouted, "Dinah, get a job! Any job!"

Each time my heart whispered, "But I still want to go to China…"

How had I, in dire financial straits, decided to go to China anyway? I prayed for guidance and my prayers were answered. I felt I could always get some kind of work, simply being a native English speaker. I also felt it would be easier to live on a shoestring budget in China than in the U.S.

In the end, I listened to my heart and went.

Xijiao Hotel and Global Village

It'd been three years since I'd last been in Beijing and I didn't know what to expect.

I was staying at the Xijiao Hotel on the outskirts of Beijing in the university district. When my mini taxi stopped in front of the new reception building, I thought, "This can't be right!" Feeling puzzled and amazed, I walked through the gleaming revolving doors into a huge open reception area with marble floors, granite counters, and an enormous crystal chandelier that hung from the high ceiling. To appreciate the contrast to the old reception building, imagine the size, look, and feel of a small-town motel front desk versus the lobby of the Waldorf Astoria in New York City, and you'd get an idea.

I did not realize it then, but this was the tip of the iceberg – an indication of the sheer magnitude of transformation that was about to take place in Beijing, and in China, in the coming decade. Truly a quantum leap!

In the three years since I was last in Beijing there'd been a growing flood of foreign students wanting to study Chinese. A Korean entrepreneur saw a need and opened a school called Global Village. Fifty-minute classes were continuously taught from 8:00 a.m. to 8:00 p.m. You could choose classes to suit your level and schedule. Such a welcome contrast to the rigid university system and program! Students flocked to the Global Village.

The school was housed in an old three-story structure with no heat or air conditioning to speak of. It was so cramped I could barely squeeze down the hall or on the stairs between classes. I'm sure it did not meet fire codes of any kind, but neither did many buildings in those days. Likely no one even noticed or was bothered by this. If you were, you would not have been in China, or studying Chinese!

I was often asked by both Chinese and foreigners why I was studying Chinese. My reply would invariably be, "Because it's my heart's desire. I love learning to speak Chinese!" The questioner often looked puzzled, as they expected my reason to be more practical, such as "It's for my work," or "So I can do business in China." They couldn't relate to moving halfway around the world, leaving family and friends, to follow a dream.

Best Deal in Beijing!

Given my scarce financial resources, I put myself on a strict student budget and ate my lunches and dinners at one of two student cafeterias. The second-floor cafeteria near the Xijiao was a huge open space with row upon row of bench tables. The first time I ate there, I went at peak mealtime and could hardly find a seat. Unlike the university cafeteria, this one housed dozens of small private vendors. The popular vendors always had a crowd of students. Sometimes you had to get pushy to get your food!

The cafeteria was not restricted to students, and there would be workers and people living in the vicinity there as well. Back in those days it was perfectly acceptable to spit chicken bones, or anything else, right on the floor! I learned to watch my step! In winter I ate with my coat on because it was freezing, literally!

Despite the unappealing conditions, there was great variety and the food was tasty! And for only US $0.65 I could get rice and two dishes. Definitely the best deal in Beijing!

New Oriental School

Finding work was very much on my mind. Soon after my arrival I learned from another foreign student about her part-time job at the New Oriental School. I immediately went there to look for Eagle, who was in charge of the oral exam program.

Eagle said, "I'll give you a try and if you work out, I'll add your name to my list of teachers." I liked this direct, no-nonsense young lady right away. The teachers were all native English speakers, and our job was to give mock oral exams to students preparing to study in Australia, England, and other European countries that required the International English Language Testing System (IELTS) oral exam.

There were usually four to six of us giving the exams at the same time. We tested four students per hour and sometimes worked eight to ten hour shifts on weekends. To be good at this, we needed to stay alert and focused, student after student. The locations for these exams were always at outlying satellite schools requiring forty-five- to sixty-minute trips in a small van.

The exam room was often a student's dorm room. A small desk would be squeezed between the bunk beds, the student sitting opposite me. There was no heat or air conditioning. In winter I'd wear leggings under my wool pants, two pairs of socks, and layered sweaters under my down coat, which I'd keep on. Unfortunately I had to take off my gloves to write! In summer I'd be perspiring in the sweltering humidity and heat!

It sounds harsh, even now, as I write this. But at the time it didn't feel harsh. This was simply part of my "new life" and new reality as a student in China. And I was very glad to have a steady source of income. We were paid between Renminbi (RMB) 80 and 110 (approximately $10 - $14US) per hour. I was soon the highest paid and received the nicest gift at Christmas. One year I was given a gift box of Starbucks coffee and a mug. It's still my favorite coffee mug!

Journal entry: February 19th, 2001

I do feel I have been trusting the process of life...overcoming, for the most part, my fear of financial lack. Somehow, Spirit will provide...

I enjoyed my brief interactions with these students from all over China. From their answers I learned much about their lives. It was heartbreaking to hear how many hated their major in college, which was forced on them by their university or their parents. They seemed so young to be feeling their lives were beyond their control.

Payday was every other week, and Eagle would meet us one by one in a room and count out our pay in RMB 100 bills. Such a great feeling holding my wad of RMB 100 notes! After a while, between this job and another one, I was able to pay most of my living expenses. Occasionally I splurged with a friend at TGIF for chicken salad and a glass of wine for RMB 100. Remember, my cafeteria meals only cost me RMB 4-5!

Which Do You Love More?

When I left for Beijing in September of 2000, I purposely did not set a timeline to return. Contrary to the way I'd lived my life all those years in the corporate world, I wanted to simply "go with the flow" and be guided by my intuition, not my analytical left brain. As I neared the end of my first year, there was no question in my mind, or heart, that I would continue my studies. My Chinese was steadily improving and I was enjoying my new adventure.

Thankfully, my mom and children understood and were supportive. Mom was in fairly good health and had my brother and his family living nearby. My son was establishing his career in southern California, and my daughter was married and living in Hong Kong at the time.

Journal entry: May 14th, 2001

I am so grateful and blessed to have good friends here...
I feel very blessed to be here.

My focus remained on studying Chinese and working as many hours as New Oriental School needed me. Partly to earn extra money, I prepared a talk which I felt would be helpful for the students as they were preparing to study abroad. My talk was titled: "Cross Cultural Communication: Perspectives of a Chinese American," pointing out the communication and cultural differences between China and western countries. The student assemblies ranged between 500-900 students! My favorite part was the Q&A.

At my first talk the question came up, "Which do you love more, China or America?" Intuitively I replied, "Which do you love more, your mom or your dad?" It was the perfect answer. They could all relate. I went on to say China is like the mother. In fact, China is often referred to as the "Motherland." The U.S. is, of course, "Uncle Sam." I concluded, "I have always considered myself so fortunate to be both Chinese and American."

Journal entry: October 6th, 2002

There are many questions about my future – sometimes I haven't a clue what the future holds – I'm learning to be comfortable with that – just trusting in Spirit to guide and provide.

Heaven and Earth Change Places

By my third year, I was becoming less intense about studying, simply enjoying being able to communicate fluently. About this time I started to do some consulting work. By 2004 I was ready to move. My physical move marked the end of a phase and the beginning of a new one; from my life as a student to that of consultant, interacting with the business community.

The government's policy in early 2000 of allowing the Chinese to purchase their own homes set off the beginning of a housing boom that dramatically changed people's lives. The magnitude of change is hard to comprehend.

Over a span of five years I was invited by a couple who were university professors to visit them in their three different apartments. Very literally, they went from "hovel to heaven," from cement floors to wooden floors, from no kitchen to a kitchen with all the modern appliances. Multiply this by millions of people moving and you'd get an idea of the changes transforming China. Once people owned their own homes, they went on a never-ending shopping spree!

When I arrived in China in 2000, there were very few cars and fewer yet privately owned. Suddenly it seemed everyone had a car and traffic jams became the new reality!

By the mid-2000s Beijing was pulling out all the stops for its debut on the world stage hosting the 2008 Olympics. The city seemed one enormous construction site! Once, standing in front of my apartment in downtown Beijing, I counted seventeen multi-story cranes in the skyline!

The Olympics allowed the world to "see" a new China emerging, one much stronger economically, more confident in itself, proud of its achievements, and ready and willing to play a larger role on the world stage.

The Chinese have a proverb, "Tian Fan Di Fu," which, literally translated, means "Heaven and Earth change places." This is the apt phrase used to describe the unprecedented transformation of China in the decade 2000-2010.

If anyone would have said to me at the outset I'd end up staying a decade in Beijing, I'd have thought it was highly improbable. As it turned out, I couldn't have planned it better if I had tried! I feel so fortunate that I was able to witness China's historic transformation firsthand.

My personal transformation was less dramatic, but deeply meaningful nonetheless. Looking back, I can better appreciate the courage and resiliency of a younger me. I grew in my faith and trust, in God and in myself. After my move and in my new role as a consultant, I was able to live much more comfortably, but I am thankful for my experience as a student. My China experiences alone could fill a book!

I always felt I'd know when the time came for me to leave China. By the spring of 2010, after an unforgettable decade, I felt my stay in China had run its course. I had realized a long-held dream: I went to China, learned the language, and reconnected with my roots.

It was time to return to my other home – home to America.

Dinah Lin, MBA, is a public speaker and author of her upcoming book, *Dare to Dream Once Again*. In it she shares stories and lessons from her own life's journey: narrowly escaping Shanghai in 1949, growing up in Ohio, raising her young family in five countries, starting her career at age thirty-six, "breaking the glass ceiling," and moving to China at age fifty-eight. Her message is "It's never too late." Learn more about Dinah at www.daretodreamonceagain.com.

~⌒~

The Voice of Truth Tells Me a Different Story

Norie A. Marfil

"Don't be afraid, I've redeemed you. I've called your name. You're mine.
When you're in over your head, I'll be there with you. When you're in
rough waters, you will not go down. When you're between a rock and a
hard place, it won't be a dead end – because I am God, your personal God,
the Holy of Israel, and your Savior. I paid a huge price for you. That's
how much you mean to me! That's how much I love you!"
~ Isaiah 43:1-4

I FOUND MYSELF IN THE OPEN Mediterranean Sea, between where I had been and where I was called to be. From darkness into light, clear blue with not a single cloud in the sky, I took my first breath and praised God that I was alive. I signaled for help, waving one of my arms in the air while going up and down in the water to stay afloat until someone from the boat eventually threw the lifesaver ring towards me.

Holding on and floating with the lifesaver ring, I turned my head around and looked back at where I had been: at the boat with some of the tourists, not that they had a clue about my almost-drowning incident, as they were too caught up in their own experiences, within their own worlds, as I was in mine. I gazed ahead towards my destination, the hot spring, and all of a sudden I heard my heart gently whisper, *"I know where we are going. It might be beyond those rocks; however, I know where we are going."* Without an inch of doubt, I took a leap of faith in spite of what had just happened to me underneath the water. With every ounce of strength left within my being, each kick of my feet into the water along with every breath, I journeyed towards the hot spring just as it was originally planned as part of the tour.

On that one fine sunny day, I was grounded in my inner knowing that I triumphed over the voice of "conniving ego," through the loving grace of God, armored by the *Voice of Truth*. I was filled with *hope, faith, unconditional love, forgiveness, healing, connections* and *trust* brought into light by a near-death and rebirth experience on July 7th, 2007, in Santorini, Greece.

Embracing and Confronting Darkness

"Once you conquer your selfish self, all your
darkness will change to light."
~ Rumi

"Is this how you are going to repay all the blessings that God has given you? You call yourself a Christian? You go to church almost every Sunday . . . you pray and pray and act all innocent, then commit the unthinkable, abortion! Wow! Some kind of Christian you are, Norie! No one will ever love you. NO ONE! Not even your dad! You don't deserve to be loved, not after this. How

could you? Shame! Shame! Shame!" echoed the constant chattering in my head. It had been a few years since I had decided to abort an unplanned pregnancy, but that hadn't been enough time for the voice to stop its loudness and mockery about how I would never be loved ever again. At some point I began to feel this to be true.

I continually heard this shameful voice, especially in the middle of the night as I lay alone in my apartment. It was also this voice, which I refer to as the "conniving ego," that spoke to me first during my near-drowning incident in Greece. When fear got ahold of me just as I was swimming towards the hot spring, it consumed my being in ways I had never imagined or experienced before… and I panicked. I found myself fighting to survive until a realization came over me that *there was nowhere to go except to embrace and confront my darkness.*

Underneath the water I had lost the concept of drowning, my location, and what day it was; it seemed that at that space, time stood still. *The only pure and true thought I was aware of was my essence, innocence, and pure existence.* Imagine being in a dream state when you are caught deeply within the experience of your dream, then waking up and trying to figure out if it was true or false.

With persuasive voice, the ego said, *"It's okay, Norie. It's okay to let go because you have lived your childhood dream. You love your parents and they love you. Your friends love you and you love them. Yes, you have made mistakes in your life, but you have learned the lessons, or at least you're trying to learn the lessons and let things go. You don't have any regrets. You know you have shortcomings, but you have learned from them. It's okay to let go."*

The ego knew that I was lost and at the lowest point of my life. It knew that I'd been running away from the hurt, pain, and shame of the abortion, going round and round with fear, and then embarking on the path of denial. The ego lingered strongly on those days while I cried my heart out. It knew to talk softly, and painted pretty pictures just to get my attention. And so I found myself agreeing with the voice that was telling me it was "okay to go" simply because I had lived my childhood dream of becoming an engineer. Besides, how could I not agree with the voice? Realizing my childhood dream was one of the biggest accomplishments in my life at the time. It hadn't always been a straight path to achieving my dream, as I had to fight with my parents, especially my mom, who had convinced me to take up nursing during my first year of college and wasn't thrilled when I instead decided to follow my childhood desire.

The ego also knew that I had come a long way in building my relationship with my parents, both agreeing to move forward with love, respect, and trust, and forgiving each other for all the hurtful things said and unsaid. It had taken many years to finally arrive at that place of knowing. It was indeed a beautiful peace of mind to know we had healed. Therefore it was not a surprise that the conniving ego would use such turning points in my life to convince me that I had lived my life – an indication to say yes to being "done" with living… period.

Convinced by the voice, I acknowledged, "Yes, I have made mistakes in my life, far worse than I could have imagined; however, I have learned from them or at least tried to. Yes, it is okay to go because I truly lived my childhood dream. Yes, it is okay to go because I know I am loved by my parents and friends, and they know that I loved them." And so I let it all go and said, "I let go of the hurt and pain, my shortcomings, and my faults. I allow and surrender everything to God: all my faults, dreams, and shortcomings… everything."

I continually repeated the words of letting go: "In my mind and in my heart, I let go and I surrender everything to God." With wide open arms I took the last possible breath I could take at the moment, and suddenly *I was no longer in pain* – no indication of hurt, shame, blame, guilt, and all the baggage of expectations I had been carrying for those years – not even the emotional pain of the abortion. They were gone.

Soon after, *I felt my entire being lift… I began to fly.* I was flying everywhere, here and there. I was in total peace and bliss.

And the conniving ego, the voice underneath the water… it vanished soon after *I surrendered, offered, and released everything to God.*

It probably knew better to be gone because of what was awaiting for me next.

Whisper of Love...
The Whisper of the Voice of Truth

"To surrender to God means to let go and just love. By affirming that love is our priority in a situation, we actualize the power of God."
~ Marianne Williamson

"In spite of it all, God, the Divine Spirit, and our Higher Self know the purity of our hearts. God forever loves and knows what we need in each moment... in each breath."
~ Journal Entry

In the midst of my internal chaos, especially when I chose to abort, I often heard a loving voice. Actually the essence of such a voice goes beyond the voice itself. Sometimes I could hear the loving whisper through songs played on the radio, the story line in a movie, a gentle hug from a friend, or even smiles from strangers. Through it all, beyond the ego-self, it was this voice that I clung to on those nights when darkness ruled my inner world... and I survived.

Underneath the water I heard another voice. *The new voice embodied unconditional love – powerful but not demanding – compassion, truth, grace, forgiveness, trust, hope, and healing all wrapped up in one.* As I became curious as to what this voice was saying, aligning myself to the voice I began to feel unconditional love come my way. I felt compassion unlike any I had ever felt before, and truth, forgiveness, and hope, one by one – I felt them all. With this profound feeling came a deeper understanding that *I was being held by the loving grace of God.* And the second voice I heard was the *Voice of Truth – the voice of God, the voice of the Divine Spirit through me, as me.*

155

Connected with the voice, I heard clearly what I was being graciously asked: *"What have you really done with your life, Norie?"* Without hesitation or questioning the query, my heart understood. But before I could respond, the loving voice added, *"What makes you think that I am done with you? I am not done with you just yet."* To which I replied, "YOU ARE RIGHT! What have I really done with my life? How selfish am I to think that I am done with my life simply because I have lived my childhood dream? Everything that I have done so far in my life was for my personal goal. But what have I really done? Nothing."

I continued, "I am afraid. I don't know where to go. Am I worthy enough to be called?" Only to be embraced by a calm response of, *"I love you and I will never leave you. I love you for you are my daughter. I love you for you are my child. Do not be afraid for I am with you. I will guide you. I will lead you. I will lead you to people who will help you be where I need you to be. ALL I NEED YOU TO DO IS TRUST ME AND WALK WITH ME."* I repeated, "I am afraid. I am afraid." And I kept on hearing, *"Trust me. Trust in me. Do not be afraid for I am with you. I have always been with you. Take my hand and I will walk with you. Take my hand and I will walk beside you all the days of your life."*

Speaking my highest truth, I proclaimed once again to God my surrender – all that I *am* and all that I am *meant to be* – and uttered in agreement, "I will walk with you. I trust in you; however, I am letting you know that I am afraid. I will walk with you and hold your hand *knowing* you are always walking beside me. I trust in you that you will lead me to people who will be my companions on the journey leading me to wherever you need me to be. *I surrender my all to you, my heart, my dreams, my truth, and my life."*

With my heart wide open, I felt someone gently and lovingly grab my hand as I slowly began the journey back from darkness into light. I WAS ALIVE!

It's Not the End – It's Only the Beginning

"I want you to know that… You are loved. You are heard.
You are seen. You are recognized. You are accepted. You are forgiven
and healed. You are never alone."
~ Journal Entry

I saw where the boat was, and it felt so close, yet so far. One by one my fellow tourists started their journey back from the water, a sign that it was almost time to return to the mainland, and so I began my own journey back to the boat. I held on tight to the lifesaver ring while kicking my feet in the water, focused and determined to reach the boat. But the more I tried to move forward, the harder I was pushed back, even farther away than where I started. Isn't it ironic how often this experience is also true in our own lives; the harder we pursue things *on our own*, the longer it takes us to get to our destination?

Faced by such irony, *I remembered* the heart-to-heart conversation I'd had with the *Voice of Truth* underneath the water. Then my heart whispered, *"We are never alone. We need help. We can't do this on our own."* Overtaken by this guidance, I looked around for the other tourists in the water until I spotted my cousin Jennifer. I began shouting. Fortunately she heard my call and agreed to pull me back safely towards the boat.

Almost seven years have passed since my near-death and rebirth experience. My journey has not always been smooth sailing, especially during those times when it requires me to revisit the "shadow" parts of myself, including the abortion. Yes, there are times when the conniving ego appears uninvited and does what it knows best; however, those are the moments I regard as indication that there's another layer of my life that needs love and surrendering to God. Through it all, I never journeyed alone in riding the waves of life, for each layer of darkness was faced, peeled, loved, surrendered, healed, and released with help.

What I hold dear in my heart in sharing this story is that I will be able to reach out to you, wherever you are on your journey, and spark love, light, and hope in your path. *And with God's unconditional love and the Voice of Truth as our companions, may we lean into the beauty of surrender and walk forward with faith, hopefulness, forgiveness, healing, openness, trust, connections, and love within our hearts.* Now, more than ever, I have a deeper knowing that my near-death and rebirth experience was meant for more than me. I do believe that it was meant for you and for anyone who comes across my story at any given moment... for my story is your story... it is our story — s*tories of God's love, amazing grace, and second chances* for us all.

This is not the end of our connection, my friend, my sister, my brother, my soul family. If anything, we've only just begun.

Norie Marfil is a walking miracle. Having survived a near-death in 2007 in Santorini, Greece, she is committed to living her divine purpose. While she's a trained engineer, Norie is also an entrepreneur, a poet at heart, and a light of hope for others. Inspired by her own struggles and healing after an abortion, she created Hearts Nest | A Soft Place to Land, where she helps others learn to focus on love rather than fear. Learn more at www.HeartsNest.com.

You Deserve to Be Right Where You Are

Sabrina Martinez

THE ADVICE IN THIS CHAPTER WILL HELP you realize that you deserve all of the accolades that have come to you.

"How in the world did I end up here?"

That's what I was thinking as I looked out over the garden of a twelfth-century French chateau. Yes, I was in France, in a real castle with a moat! Being here wasn't bad, just unlikely for someone who grew up where I did. Back then I never would have pictured myself in a place like this.

I was here as a member of a strategic planning team from Swarthmore College in Pennsylvania. The others on the team were brilliant, successful, and wealthy. They were PhDs, corporate presidents, lawyers, authors, professors… and then there was me – none of the above.

I had been on the college's board of managers with this team for two years and feelings of insecurity were my constant companion at our meetings. The only reason I felt able to contribute to the conversation at board meetings was because our board materials were sent in advance and I was able to prepare. My mantra was, "They might be smarter, but no one will work harder or prepare more than I will."

But this week-long retreat would consist of brainstorming and exercises to get us thinking outside of the box. Without the ability to prepare in advance, I worried that my biggest fear would come true: they would discover I wasn't really smart enough to be among them.

Insecurity hadn't plagued me my entire life. I grew up in a poor neighborhood, in a rented house with my mother, my grandmother, and my older sister. My grandmother cleaned houses and my mother was a receptionist. Occasionally my mom would take on extra jobs to buy Christmas or birthday presents. I never knew my father. It didn't seem strange that my sister and I didn't have a father, as many of the kids in our neighborhood didn't have one for one reason or another. At two I began attending Head Start, a government-sponsored early childhood education program for poor and underserved children. I also qualified for free lunch. In those days it never felt like we were poor because the whole neighborhood was in the same situation. We were just like everyone else.

For most of my scholastic career I actually felt I was always one of the smartest people in the room. Because I was one of the smart kids I felt like a big fish in our small pond. I got A's in all of my classes. I was the captain of the volleyball team and the vice-president of my class. Socioeconomic class didn't seem to have any bearing on success. Any and every goal was within my reach because I worked hard and was smart. If I wanted to go on a class trip and we didn't have the money, I'd organize a fundraiser. If I didn't like the grades one teacher gave me, I'd ask another teacher to give me a second opinion. The extent of my confidence knew no limits. From grades to goals, I thought I could do it all.

Then I went to Swarthmore College. That is where I first learned that socioeconomic class made a huge difference in the broader world. It wasn't visually obvious, nor was it blatant; it was just subtle things that let me know that I was different. My classmates had traveled around the world, had summer houses, and went on ski trips for winter break or to Martha's Vineyard for spring break. They also came to college with AP credits, spoke multiple languages, played several instruments, and had paid internships. There were even two Jeopardy Teen Champions in my freshman class.

My first year at Swarthmore I gave Christmas cards to all of my friends, including my Jewish friends. I realized my mistake when one friend pulled me aside and laughingly explained that Jews don't celebrate Christmas. A classmate, whose surname was also Martinez, proclaimed that I was a disgrace to my Hispanic heritage because I didn't speak Spanish. I had only ever thought of myself as black. That was the first time I considered that I was also Hispanic. It was also the first and only time I felt ashamed of growing up without a father.

Academics were also a challenge at Swarthmore. I chose to study engineering. To say that engineering at Swarthmore was hard is an understatement. Nearly eighty percent of the sixty-four students who started in engineering my freshman year dropped out. At graduation only fourteen of us remained. We started with seven women in engineering and four years later only two of us graduated. Classes had to be graded on a curve. I remember getting tests back in class and holding my breath until the professor wrote the curve scale on the board. Most of the grades I received in my engineering courses were C's... a far cry from the A's I got in high school. I did take several liberal arts classes because they were graduation requirements. I felt the A's I received in those classes were insignificant. Instead I focused on the C's I got in engineering, discounted the A's and wondered if I really belonged at Swarthmore.

I graduated in four years with an engineering degree, but never felt like I actually earned my diploma. I was sure that it was only luck that got me through the program. If I hadn't had my study group, my senior project advisor, or all of the other blessings that made the situation bearable, I wouldn't have made it.

Following graduation, my self-esteem rebounded. I landed a great job and purchased a condominium in New Jersey. I made some great friends and went on to get my MBA from the University of Michigan, Ross School of Business. At graduation, I even had sixteen job offers! I then moved to Houston, Texas, and purchased my second home. I ran the Anchorage Alaska Marathon, started public speaking, and leading Passino Test workshops. I also began volunteering with AVANCE-Houston, Theater under the Stars, United Way, and many other wonderful organizations. Life was good.

Even with all the success I experienced, I still had a reoccurring dream that I had to take an engineering exam and was not prepared. Another frequent nightmare was that I received a call from Swarthmore telling me that my diploma was not valid and I had to give it back. My insecurity about Swarthmore kept me from returning to campus for almost fifteen years after graduating.

In 2005 I was elected to the Swarthmore Alumni Council. I honestly didn't think I was making much of a contribution. I went to meetings, spoke up when I had something to say, and did the team assignments. I was shocked when in my second year on the council I was asked to be part of the executive committee and lead the Student Support Working Group! I accepted the position though I was certain there were more qualified candidates.

Again, I didn't do anything extraordinary when leading my team. I just planned the meetings and asked team members to take accountability for projects and events. Every working group chair was doing a great job running their group. In fact, other working groups did some very impactful projects during our two-year term. Once again I was surprised when I was asked to be the president of the alumni council and the alumni association. As president of the alumni association, I would also have a seat on the college's board of managers. I humbly accepted the position though again I was sure there was probably a better choice.

My executive committee was a rock star team! My team included several professors, a school principal, a state senator, an emergency room physician, and the president of the US Peace Corps Association. I was honored to lead this esteemed group. Knowing the working groups were in such great hands, I had fun implementing council engagement projects like the Thank You project where we contacted current donors to thank them for their contributions to the college and give them updates about campus activities. The new president of the college came on during my term, and I had the opportunity to welcome her on behalf of all alumni at her inauguration. One of the most meaningful things I did during my tenure as council president was to create the Alumni Council Impact Award and present it to the first recipient, Eugene (Gene) Lang, Swarthmore's largest donor. When I had a rare opportunity to speak with Gene, he shared with me how important he felt it was to recognize people and let them know how much you appreciated their contribution. I took those words to heart and decided in that moment I would do my best to always recognize people while they can know how much I appreciate them. Swarthmore gave Gene a banquet honoring his many contributions to the college. I was proud that I got to present the award and rename it the Eugene Lang Impact Award in front of his friends and family.

Because the engagement of the alumni council was higher than ever, the board chair declared my term as president as a huge success. For that reason I was asked to participate on the strategic planning team, and that is how I ended up in the French chateau, doubting my abilities and feeling like I didn't belong. I discounted all that I had accomplished in my lifetime, and doubted that my contribution on this team would even matter.

While I was standing in the gigantic dining room looking out over the garden, one of the other team members, a Swarthmore professor, joined me. She asked about my experience at Swarthmore. I hesitantly shared my thoughts about feeling ill prepared for Swarthmore's rigorous curriculum and the difference my socioeconomic background made both academically and socially. I even shared about the recurring dream that my diploma was taken back. I shared all of this somehow feeling that by exposing myself it would be less embarrassing than being discovered as a fraud on the team. She then asked, "If the team is so brilliant, how is it possible that you were able to fool everyone for the past two years?" I didn't have an answer. She followed up: "If Swarthmore was such a struggle for you, why do you continue to volunteer?" Again, I didn't have an answer and remained silent. She continued to lecture me about feeling worthy. I'll summarize that advice for you.

Listen to Others. When people say good things about you, believe them. What would they have to gain from being untruthful about your good qualities? How often do you go out of your way to give insincere compliments? Chances are that others are just as sincere in their assessment of you. Beyond listening, resist any negative response that you have to a compliment. Just absorb the compliment and say thank you.

Stop Comparing Yourself to Others. Think about the value that you bring to the team. Perhaps you are the youngest, the only woman, or of a different race or socioeconomic background. That makes you unique. You are able to see the situation in a different way because of your distinctive life experiences. Use your perspective to your advantage and present a different point of view.

See Others Objectively. Just as you have strengths and shortcomings, remember others have them too. You don't have to revel in their shortcomings, but objectively seeing their shortcomings may make them less intimidating.

Be Authentic. If you're nervous, let others know about your anxiety. You don't have to announce it from the front of the room, rather connect with someone individually. You might create an ally. You might also find that they are nervous too.

Think Positively. Write down a positive affirmation to combat the negative statements that keep entering your mind. For example if you think "I'm not as successful as they are," write down positive affirmations like "I belong here," "I earned this," and "I have a unique perspective." It might not feel authentic at first, but write them down, post them where you can see them, and repeat them to yourself multiple times each day.

Review Your History. Think about the last time you had these doubts. Chances are the situation ended well. A success probably led you here, so take a minute to acknowledge that success rather than feeling the same old fear.

Fake It Until You Make It. You don't have to wait until you feel confident to act confidently. Courage comes from taking risks. The more you do it, the easier it becomes.

Be Realistic. Ask yourself, "What is the worst that can happen?" "What am I really afraid of?" "What is the worst-case scenario?" and "Is that outcome completely unbearable?" Chances are what you are most afraid of isn't really that horrible.

Good, Better, Best. Now that you have imagined the worst that can happen, imagine something good that can happen, something better that can happen, and the best thing that can happen. Be outrageous with these thoughts. If nothing else, this will put a smile on your face.

Stay in the Moment. Stay present and listen to or better yet participate in the conversation in the room. When you stop listening to the conversation going on in your head you will find your doubts disappear.

Visualize Success. What does success look like to you? What outcome would you like? What will have to happen for you to pat yourself on the back and say, "Job well done"? Focus on that outcome and the steps you can take to make it come true. If a journey of a thousand miles begins with a single step, a journey to a successful outcome begins with a single action.

Congratulate Yourself. Take time to breathe, then list all of your wins. Too often we focus on the things that didn't go the way we wanted them to. Yes, acknowledge those things and think about how you can improve next time, but be sure to document your successes and congratulate yourself for those as well.

Though the conversation wasn't a tidy list of twelve tips as it appears above, it was a turning point for me, especially in my volunteer work with Swarthmore. The retreat was a great success. I was also asked to remain on the board for another year to lead the alumni engagement stream of the strategic planning process. Most important, I still have friends from my time on the board that I am in touch with to this very day.

I think back on this pep talk whenever I begin to doubt myself. I hope if you ever find yourself in a situation in which you're feeling undeserving or out of place, that you, too, will think back on this chapter and realize that you really do deserve to be right where you are.

According to Einstein, the meaning of life is "service to others." International speaker and author **Sabrina Martinez** lives by those words. A passionate volunteer, she spends countless hours making a difference using her experience in human resources and communications to serve as a community leader in education, the arts, and services for the blind. Whether volunteering or speaking to a crowd, Sabrina credits service as the secret to her success. Visit www. SabrinaMartinez.com for more information.

Transforming My Aging Script

Sharon Matthias

It started on December 17th. I remember being curious that morning.
"So I'm sixty-five.
I wonder what today will bring."

I WAS CURIOUS BECAUSE TURNING SIXTY-FIVE is a pretty undesirable portal in our society. Simply by passing through this gate you move directly from being active and productive to being dependent and a burden – at least the way we calculate population statistics sees it this way. The World Bank calculates the *total dependency ratio* as "the ratio of dependents – people younger than fifteen or older than sixty-four, to the working-age population – those aged fifteen to sixty-four." Some refer to it as "representing the burden on productive members of a society."

What a statistic! The imbedded assumptions are staggering! In addition to the reality that in today's world lots of people younger than fifteen or older than sixty-four are working, note the negative assumptions!

- First, that making a productive contribution to society is totally reliant on whether you work or not

- Second, if you're not working, you're totally DEPENDENT

- And, if you're dependent, you're a BURDEN on the productive members of society

Sixty-five is also the age at which Canadian residents' government pensions can kick in. Not so long ago, before 2011, people could still legally be required to retire from positions and life work simply because they had turned sixty-five. So becoming a pensioner meant you had to give up something that defined your identity. Even if you didn't find your job particularly meaningful, before age sixty-five you had an answer to the usual question "And what do you do for a living?"

I saw the magic of this number impacting my friends and colleagues. A close friend was so resistant that she refused to sign the forms required to get her pension benefits. Her husband finally filled the papers out and stood over her until she signed them so he could mail them. I hear the phrase "I'm just getting old" fall mindlessly off the lips of friends, colleagues, and strangers in grocery store lines as the automatic source of any problem.

I was also curious because I wondered whether that birthday would be different. Birthdays haven't been a big hurdle for me. Unlike others in my network of friends and family, forty, fifty, even sixty passed without particular distress. If anything, my life got better as I travelled more journeys around the sun.

I spent my sixty-fifth birthday in pretty much the same way as any other birthday. The sky didn't fall and the roof didn't cave in. As near as I could tell I was pretty much the same the day after as I had been the day before. I assumed that I'd gotten through that one with equal ease.

But not so fast! Perhaps I wasn't going to escape after all! As the year wore on, I began to recognize that my thoughts were rolling a movie that promised worse and worse futures. It didn't seem to matter what the provocation was – a concern over cash flow, noticing a new ache in my body (or even an old familiar one), or a casual comment from someone about how aging was affecting them set off dire thoughts.

Whatever the stimulus, the result was an automatic mental movie of me in a small room with the ceiling closing in and becoming darker by the moment, huddled in a chair with no company and no money. Even more frightening was the lack of freedom; I wasn't in control and didn't have any options for weathering sudden changes in my world. And this catastrophe seemed imminent – just a moment in time away. In fact, since my mental movies play in Technicolor, 3D, and SurroundSound, it was like it was happening right then! Not good!

It took me a while to "wake up" and move into action, though that didn't help much at first. I'm a problem solver by nature, yet it seemed no matter how I argued with myself about the likelihood of the movie happening, I could not stop it from playing automatically in my mind. I reminded myself that even though my very small pension and Registered Retirement Savings Plan (RRSP) wouldn't support me in my current lifestyle (a serious bummer!), I wouldn't starve. However unappealing it might be, in a pinch, and with a little research and creativity, a move to a living situation with lower overhead was clearly feasible. (My main requirement was a high-speed internet connection!)

And I had time. My current projects meant I was booked for at least six months to a year, so realistically I had time to develop transition plans even if I assumed that I would need to live on a lower income in the future. I might not like the view or the neighborhood, but I wouldn't be stuck in a tiny room with no heat or lights, or in physical danger. The mental movie that I was creating in my head was clearly not reasonable… but that didn't make it stop.

I've learned that one of the most important things I can do to create my quality of life and state of health is to be conscious about my thoughts – the movie running in my head. That movie wasn't my idea of a healthy or desirable story. As I began to realize that it was playing at least once a day, I got more fearful and more frustrated! Gradually I was able to hit pause, even momentarily, stand back a bit, and at least ask myself why the constant catastrophizing, and why so strong now when my life was running along pretty well?

And if not that movie, then what was the alternative? What movie did I WANT playing in my head? I loved my work and had a vibrant consulting practice. I had no desire to stop working, to retire in the classic sense of only gardening, golf, and grandkids. But beyond staying engaged in meaningful activities that made a difference in the world, I didn't have much clarity about how that was going to be achieved if I didn't want to keep working at the same pace I had been.

What to do now? So I did what I often do. I asked everyone I could about how they thought aging worked. When I'm stuck with a dilemma, this is my best action. I've found lots of good and innovative ideas come of this practice. I don't limit myself to my immediate circle; I'm too likely to get ideas that mirror my own. When I'm on a search like this I need lots of disruptive ideas! I find ways to engage lots of people in casual conversation – in cabs, grocery store lines, and hair salons, as well as with my friends and colleagues.

I found others were asking much the same question. Then one person talked of something they called an "aging script" – the automatic assumptions we create unconsciously as we grow up. Our aging script comes from parents, friends, colleagues, the movies, newspapers, and magazines – the unconscious and untested absorption of others' expectations. Wow! My movie certainly had a non-generative aging script! So I started to pay attention to my movie as a script that I could rewrite if I chose.

For about the last thirty years I've gotten better at living my life more and more in ways that align with something Ralph Waldo Emerson wrote: "All life is an experiment. The more experiments you make the better." I was trained in a discipline that involved lab work, so I understand the world of experimentation from that angle. But for life experiments, I don't need a white lab coat or even those protective goggles. To live life as a learning lab, all I need is an open mind, to ask if something has to be this way, and to be willing to frame things in a new light. Oh yes, and to be willing to risk being "wrong" or "flaky" so I can expand the possible solution space as broadly as possible.

Experimenting with a conscious aging script became my priority. Different options became mental experiments. I could play them out to check against what I had learned about what I'm likely to do and enjoy in life.

Options came from watching others and also from memories. I remembered asking people a few years earlier how they decided whether someone they met was forty-five or sixty. The best answer I got was from a young esthetician during my pedicure. After a few moments of silence (I got the sense this wasn't a question she'd been asked before), she ventured that in her experience, people who were forty-five were looking ahead and talking about future possibilities. People who were sixty only talked about their memories and past achievements. Amazing! This had nothing to do with physical experience and gave me a fabulous clue. I added "making future dreams and plans" and "expansive, not limiting or contracting" to my desirable aging script.

So what else would a desirable aging script include? I didn't expect to create an aging script that required a forty-year-old body. I knew there were physiological changes that go with aging, though I noticed that some people seemed more impacted than others. However, you'll have recognized that I engage with the world mentally as much as physically. I also knew that the world of neuroscience is providing new insights about brain plasticity, and fields like psychoneuroimmunology demonstrate a mind-body connection that's different than my early schooling suggested was possible. So I was prepared to test out the possibility that changing my mental movie would influence my physical state in some positive way. At least, I figured, a different movie would help me live with diminished physical capacity with joy and sanguinity.

I experimented with my thoughts. What would happen if my movie involved growth and development, not just resting on what I'd achieved? What was my next adult development stage to grow into?

But I also argued with myself about whether *growth and development* and *aging* really could be in the same sentence!

That part of the process was like imagining possibilities when transitioning from high school, but now I had not only my formal education to build on but knowledge gained from a lot of years of some very exciting and fascinating experiences. Above all, what legacy did I still have to live besides sharing what I'd already learned? What did I still want to create?

Interestingly, the old limiting movie started to sputter. And when I turned sixty-six a year later, it wasn't playing nearly as often, nearly as loudly, or nearly as automatically. And best of all, I was catching it more and more quickly to re-correct. My new movie, one of a future with vitality, ongoing engagement and contribution, productivity, creativity, and dreams was gaining momentum.

Though I still have relapses, my new movie has since strengthened even further and it's getting more comfortable as I live into it. I have a future as well as a past. While I celebrate my past accomplishments, I'm no longer limited by them. I can imagine making future contributions in a variety of different ways. The path I will finally settle on is not yet completely clear, but I more often get glimpses of what I am becoming.

I decided recently to change my terminology from an "aging script" to a "living script." Since aging and dying are normal parts of living, at the very least it seems to me that calling it a living script is more likely to be disruptive; I'm more likely to remain conscious of what movie I'm playing and keep the script one of engagement and growth. And I'm more likely to live life in such a way that younger people say, "How wonderful it must be to be that age."

Seven-Stage Cycle for Transforming Your "Mental Aging Script"

Transformation isn't a one-shot deal in my life. *Transforming* is perhaps a better word since it is one-step-at-a-time work for me.

An event or situation happens, and I thrash about in the surprises it creates, reacting and resisting reality. Finally I come to enough peace with it that I can make choices about whether I'll change the thinking that underlies my behavior or the way I make sense of my experience.

As I look back now, although it's a pretty messy process, it seems as though there were seven stages in a repeating cycle for purposefully transforming my recurring movie to one that expects aging to be a positive experience:

1. **Paying attention** to the picture, movie, or audio playing in my head, and **recognizing and naming** it as a storyline

2. **Deciding** whether it is serving me, and **choosing** to continue or to change it

3. **Imagining** a range of options and gradually narrowing them down to the script I'd choose to write, one that supports my desired version of who I am becoming. (Having more options gives me choice and personal power.) This is helped by **remembering** past examples in my life when my mind played tricks on me, leading me to believe in dire circumstances, and when I or others found different possible ways to think about the situation.

4. **Paying attention**, catching myself as many times as I can during the day, and taking a moment to remind myself that there are other options. Then practicing what the new script would play out like. Even saying to myself, "That's not the only option!" in the moment helps to pause or stop the script.

5. **Habituating** – gradually becoming more comfortable and confident with a script that sees positive possibilities in aging, even if that includes diminishment of physical abilities

6. **Continuing to grow and develop** – keeping watch to see if the script needs further refinement, updating, or revising to imbed new possibilities that have emerged

7. **Repeat.** Watch to see how I'm doing. The feedback loops help me be conscious about whether to change something in my process.

Earlier in life I was habituated to assuming I was a victim of outside forces, so I had to work to transform that script first. I appreciate that I'm better at living one of my tag lines – "We design our future with every decision we make – whether in life or in policy and program design. Our choice is whether we make our decisions purposefully."

Baby boomers have changed the world in every age stage we've experienced. What are we going to do with this one? Perhaps my story will spark you to pay attention to your own aging script and consider whether it serves you. Perhaps it will create a small crack in your assumptions that aging has to be the way society usually says it is.

And hopefully it helps convince you that collectively we need to reconsider what it means to be a productive member of society; that it doesn't just depend on working, and it isn't limited to ages fifteen to sixty-four!

Sharon Matthias, the "Pragmatic Provocateur," is passionate about figuring out how the world works. As a trusted professional consultant, she supports leaders in designing major public systems that help people create more meaningful lives and a world that really does work. Also a mother, grandmother, and friend, she thrives on learning from experience and investing in her own adult development. You can learn more about Sharon at www.PositionsOfInfluence.com and get her Provocateur Paper "Can Aging Be an Opportunity?"

Happily Ever After: From "Perfect" to Purpose

Carin Rockind

I CROUCHED ON THE FLOOR, HANDS OVER MY HEAD. "Please don't hurt me! Please don't hurt me!" I could hear myself screaming. I peeked to the side and looked up at my predator. The gun was now pointed at my head and tears began streaming down my cheeks.

Moments earlier I had been blabbing on the phone with my sister. I had just been on an awful first date – the first "first" date in a long time. It was July 24th, 2008, and this date was desperate action to relieve my depression. Why I thought that a blind date would make me feel better, I have no idea, but it was providing a great laugh. "He smelled!" I laughed to my sister as I put my key into my condo door. "And the WORST sense of humor!"

Suddenly I felt a presence behind me, nearly on top of me. Hot, heavy breath blanketed my neck. I spun around and found myself nose-to-nose with my predator's sad eyes. I gasped.

"Are you going inside?" I asked him, hoping he was just visiting a friend who lived in my building. His soft eyes bore into mine, and then they looked down at the gun he was holding to my belly.

"AHHH!!" I screamed and fell to the floor. I could hear my heartbeat pounding… bump, bump, bump. I could feel sweat dripping down my face. My brain flooded with images of the people I loved – my parents, my siblings, my niece, my grandparents, my friends. My heart sank as I asked God to tell them goodbye. I thought of my travels to Paris, Russia, Israel, and Asia, and felt grateful I had seen the world. I then remembered everything I had not yet done. The books I wanted to write but never had. The lectures I yearned to give, but didn't. The people I wanted to impact who would never hear my story. The life purpose I was meant to fulfill, but wouldn't. I had been too scared. I found excuse after excuse about health insurance and income and prestige. I got wrapped up in which graduate program to take instead of simply choosing one and going for it. I allowed myself to pretend that men would make my dreams go away. I became paralyzed by fear of rejection, fear of not making it, fear of finding out that I wasn't a good writer after all. But in that moment those fears seemed irrelevant. What was the fear for if I was going to end up dying on my condominium floor? I desperately wanted a second chance. So in that moment I pleaded to God. "If you let me live, I promise to pursue that purpose you gave me. I promise."

And at that moment the man took my purse and ran.

The "Perfect" Life

Years earlier I had been hungry for purpose. I'd "had it all" – my tall, dark-haired, attorney husband; our beautifully manicured home; our pure-bred golden retriever; and a rising corporate marketing career. I made gourmet Thanksgiving meals for our family and hosted barbecues for our friends. Life looked as I'd always dreamt it would: perfect. All by the time I was twenty-four.

Somehow, though, I felt miserable in my so-called perfect life. The walls caved in on my spirit and my throat choked on our suburban air. I cried almost every day. "What's wrong *with you?*" my husband would ask. "Look around." He would point to our hardwood floors and brick fireplace. "We're happy."

When I was a little girl, I had dreamt of this life. My cousin Stacy and I would play with Barbies in my bedroom. We each had a pretend Barbie's Dream House and a beautiful Ken, and we lived next to each other. We wanted this life for good reason. My parents have been blissfully married for forty-nine years, while Stacy's dad had died when she was four. We saw the struggles her mom went through, and though I'm not sure we were conscious of it as little girls, deep down we understood that we didn't want to be alone.

I was so afraid to be alone that I went to college looking for my husband. I had come out of an abusive relationship in high school and couldn't wait to get away. In college I could start over. I could meet my man and we would live happily ever after. As planned, I met Mike during my freshman year, and he was everything I had wanted: tall, handsome, muscular, and on his way to becoming a lawyer. He wooed me with flowers delivered to my dorm room, took me out to expensive dinners, and put poems under my pillow. He was perfect husband material, and I was madly in love. We got married the day before my twenty-third birthday, and I thought that was the end of the story: we'd live happily ever after, like *Cinderella*. It's not that I was naïve – I was hopeful.

But we didn't live happily ever after. Turns out that those flowers and expensive dinners were put on credit cards, and I was suddenly $40,000 in debt the day I got married. He insisted that he manage the money because he was the man. We disagreed about money, religion, family, and how to spend our free time.

Plus, I wanted more. My soul needed energy, passion, freedom. I begged to move to a city. As a child I had dreamt of being on stage, under the lights. And even though I couldn't dance or sing, I hungered for the excitement. I felt like I had a higher purpose. I yearned to do something meaningful and make a difference. Instead I just felt caged. So we fought. And when we fought we hit below the belt. It was loud and ugly inside our perfect home.

There Is More

I was too afraid to talk about it, so I cried in the shower where my husband couldn't hear me. One day I consoled myself beneath the hot streams of water: "It's okay, Car." I hugged myself like a little girl. "I guess this is all there is to life." To which an older, calmer voice responded, "Oh, no. There is much more." I looked up at wherever this voice was coming from. No one was there but me. "There is?" I whispered to myself. Softly, strongly, the voice responded, "Yes, Honey, there is." My heart filled with warmth. I sheepishly smiled, nodded, and stepped out of the shower. I didn't know what my next step would be, but I had the first bit of comfort that I had felt in a long time. I knew that everything was going to be okay.

What I now know is that my married, corporate life felt empty, meaningless, and misaligned. My ex and I did "have" a lot, but I lacked that rich, satisfying feeling that comes from living with purpose. I lacked the gratification that comes from making the world a better place. I lacked the fulfillment that comes from contributing the depths of our souls to enhance others' lives. I lacked the freedom we feel when we expand our wings and soar. I desperately wanted to not just make money, but make an impact.

Somewhere deep down I knew there was more to life. *There had to be.*

Another year would pass until my husband and I got divorced, and another ten years until I followed my purpose as a career. But that day in the shower represented a very important moment: the first step on my path to purpose.

Uncovering Purpose

On one hand, I felt great relief when I got divorced. On the other, I felt an enormous amount of self-doubt and shame. I had built my life upon a perfect picture, so without it, who was I? I knew what I *didn't* want – but what *did* I want? I had no clue. Freedom is wonderful, but it can also be overwhelming and lonely.

Fortunately a chance encounter showed me my path. It was March 3rd, my grandpa's birthday. He always went to synagogue, and I had nothing better to do that day so I decided to surprise him there. As I walked into the sanctuary, my heart leapt. Sitting behind my grandfather was my former high school youth group advisor, Ida. I hadn't seen her in ten years. I pulled her into the hallway and shed tears on her shoulder as she held me. "Go volunteer," she said. "Call the youth group tomorrow and become an advisor." She could have told me to jump off the Empire State Building and I would have done it, but instead she gave me the greatest gift of my life: my true joy.

Through the youth group girls, I came alive. These girls were full of hope, optimism, and dreams. They could do anything and be anything, and I wanted to encourage them to follow their *own* paths. But many of them were also insecure. They felt ugly, fat, insignificant, and unworthy. Three of them had eating disorders. Another cut herself to numb the pain. They were my mirror – every pain I felt inside, every truth of my inner beauty, every insecurity I had was showcased in these girls. But all I saw was their beauty. Where they noticed their imperfections, I marveled at their uniqueness. In each one of them I saw a specific combination of strength, creativity, and charm. Each had distinct gifts, and I had the gift of seeing them. Inspiring them to love themselves made my skin tingle. Encouraging them to feel worthy made my blood race with joy. Empowering them to pursue their dreams was a natural high. I wanted more.

The Rocky Path

I now understood that my purpose was to empower women, but I could not figure out how to turn it into a career. It was 2001, and I had never heard of life coaching. Plus, I really wanted to move the masses.

At first I took my purpose literally. "Maybe I should work for the youth group," I thought, "or become a high school teacher." But I didn't want to teach English, I wanted to inspire self-love. Friends would say, "You want to be the Jewish Oprah!" Yes!... but how does one do that? And who would hire me anyhow? I didn't have a degree in journalism or psychology. I was no one — just a divorced twenty-eight-year-old with a big dream. Join the club, Lady.

I yearned to serve, but lived in agony. Self-doubt spun around and around in my head, ultimately paralyzing me into a deep depression. Eventually I decided that a relationship would fix my problems. I found men who were just like my husband. Different name, same golf shirt. I took higher paying corporate jobs, trying to convince myself that I was making an impact. In one automotive marketing job I reasoned that wheels keep a car on the road, which keeps families safe. It was true, but pathetically off-purpose.

Eventually I got a VP title, made six figures, and bought myself a convertible and a boat. The golden handcuffs gripped tightly. So did my anxiety. My stress became so great that I got shingles at the ripe age of thirty-four. I beat myself into a pulp every night. The shame was too much to bear. How could I have left my marriage only to end up stuck and afraid again? I hated every inch of my cowardly body. Over time I begged a psychiatrist for medication. I needed something – *anything* – to numb the pain.

A Second Chance

That night on my condo floor, with the gun held to my head, I got what I needed: a second chance at life.

Not even one year later, a friend whom I hadn't seen in twenty years sent me a message on Facebook: "You're always so positive, have you seen this?" It was a link to the University of Pennsylvania and their master's degree in the new field of positive psychology – the scientific study of happiness. As I read through the program and dove into the research, my heart leapt and my eyes welled. I had finally found my path. Sometimes it takes a near-death experience to realize you'd barely been living.

Approximately one year later, on September 8th, 2010, I began graduate school at UPenn. It was Rosh Hashanah, the Jewish New Year, the holiday of new beginnings. It was also my thirty-sixth birthday. In Hebrew, thirty-six means "two lives." Indeed, I'd been given a second life.

Purpose Is True Happiness

Since that day I have dedicated myself to inspiring, encouraging, and empowering women to break free from whatever binds them to uncover and live their purpose. No dream is too big; no desire too silly; no hope too naïve. Will I be "Oprah"? No. I am me. And I'm the only one with my specific strengths, wisdom, and quirks to share. Yes, I teach happiness on the radio, on TV, on stages worldwide, but I also do so in my living room and at my dinner table. Purpose is no longer a career path; it's how I live every day. Purpose is not a job title or even a role like being a parent. It is a verb. It is how I actively impact the world. And by "world" I mean my family, community, and circle of influence.

So who are you? What is juicy and special and beautiful about you? What are those secret dreams inside of you begging to be set free? No one has your specific set of strengths, talents, passions, and wisdom, so you are the only one who can live your purpose. The secret to happiness is allowing your full self to be seen, even what you consider to be imperfections. You've probably walked through worse pain before — the pain of defeat, of suffocation, of shame. These are just badges of strength and fuel for purpose.

You don't have to leave your marriage like I did. You don't have to leave your loftily titled six-figure job like I did. And God willing, you will not be held up at gunpoint like I was. Rather, decide to release the paralyzing fear that is getting in your way. Break free from old beliefs that no one will want to hear what you have to say and you can't make enough money living your purpose. Rewrite thoughts that say you're not good enough, pretty enough, or worthy. You are more than worthy; you are needed. It's time to break free from believing that living your purpose is irresponsible, selfish, or stupid. I can think of nothing more responsible, selfless, or wise than impacting others with your unique gift.

Are you ready to step forward?

Carin Rockind is a powerful international speaker, trainer, and women's empowerment coach. After fifteen years as a corporate exec, she traded in her suits to pursue her purpose. She combines her expertise in positive psychology with wisdom from surviving abuse, divorce, and crime to teach women to move past fear and contribute their gifts to the world. She is SiriusXM's Happiness Guru and Dr. Oz's Motivation Expert for young women. For tips and tools, visit www.PurposeGirl.com.

Embracing Fear in Its Many Guises

Melissa Rowe, PCC, MSW

I WAS IN MY FIFTIES WHEN I WAS SHAKEN BY tremendous awakenings which revealed to me that I must first love and take care of myself before helping and giving to others. I cannot change what has happened in the past; however, I can change my perception and reaction to those events. I must become a friend to myself through respect, honesty, and unconditional self-love.

Although in the past I allowed fear to dictate most of my life decisions, this awakening carried a different type of fear – a consciousness of my deeper sense of knowing. So to see where I had been and self-assess my now, I pulled out my lessons about fear. There were five of them.

First, I had come to understand fear as a natural and continuous process of growth and change.

Second, I had done the work and faced the fact that the only way to get rid of my fear of doing something was to just do it.

Third, I realized that the only way to feel better and stronger about myself and my capabilities was to "feel the fear and do it anyway."

Fourth, pushing through fears is less frightening than living with the underlying feeling of helplessness.

Fifth, I recognized that the problem is not fear itself, but rather how I identify and handle it. One of the ways I have learned how to handle fear is to move myself from positions of pain to positions of power. It took almost a lifetime to learn this, but I honor myself now when I acknowledge how my personal awakening was built on a manufactured courage and inner strength. I created it and lived it, and for me this process worked.

When I looked back on my life, I recognized that each challenge gave me all I needed to create greater experiences. This occurred in stages, too. In stage one I wanted a greater sense of belonging, but my mind did not really believe that I deserved more. Ironically, in stage two, I became attached to a status quo I had created, and did not trust myself to risk experiencing anything other than what I already knew. Stage three of this growth from various challenges was acknowledging that I did not trust life to bring me the rewards that I desired, and I did not trust that I would be able to handle whatever came my way.

Abandonment and fear have been prominent constants throughout my life. My main fear was that I would be abandoned by people. This theme ran my life. When I was sixteen, my mother grew tired of her husband's physical and emotional abuse and left in the middle of the night. I recall how our neighbors helped her get away. Being the oldest child, I assumed the adult role of caretaker and nurturer for my siblings and my father. I was of course unprepared for this role, and most of all unprepared for becoming a replacement for my mother in relation to my father. This had a lasting, detrimental impact on my life. I felt abandoned and betrayed. As I put the needs of others before my own, all my decisions were made for me by others, and there was no opportunity to share what I felt.

Mother's absence lasted eighteen months. She signaled her return home on the condition that my father would no longer be there. Consequently he emigrated to the United Kingdom, and thus I was abandoned again. Two years later I left my home in our small village in the western part of Jamaica for the big city of Kingston. I needed to work to support my mother and younger siblings. I was eighteen.

My real quest began in my late twenties. I journeyed from Jamaica to Ottawa, Canada, looking for that "savior" opportunity. I didn't know who I was, what I could be, or where I would go. I was programmed to be compliant, predictable, and easy to get along with. I worked hard and sent money home for food and clothes and to keep a roof over my family's head, all the while feeling that something was missing and believing I was "second place." I lived large parts of my life believing I was not good enough and that I had to do everything and be everything to everyone else.

As my constant companion, fear of life itself cycled through my mind and reinforced old thoughts, hour by hour, minute by minute. There were times when I became paralyzed. My initiative seemed swallowed by the habit of allowing others to define me. I discovered that fear can make it impossible to see the light ahead. It woke me to how tired, isolated, and unfulfilled I felt. I was drowning in my tears. I began asking myself, "Is this all there is to life? What do I want for my life?"

Because I didn't know, life had an answer for me. I became pregnant at twenty-eight, and my partner wanted me to have an abortion. Instead, I dropped him and became a single mother. There was a power within me that I did not know existed. I considered myself whole and complete without him. What I did was turn the tables – I abandoned someone, an intimate with whom I shared life – much as I had been abandoned by my parents.

Years later, during my marriage to a different man, abandonment issues resurfaced. With my husband's continuous overseas travels, I felt as though I was again a single parent. I was, in fact, but the children were grown, and it was my inner child that was left alone again.

I realized there were different aspects of me that I could share with others. At times I experienced a fear so deep it left me immobilized. I took time out to look at what I was bumping up against. I discovered I had spent a great deal of time waiting for someone to rescue me, honor me, and fulfill my dreams. This waiting had become a running theme in my life. I waited for my mother to come back; waited for my father to take care of me as his little girl; waited for my husband to come back from his travels to be my husband and partner. I was constantly waiting to truly trust and believe the power within, honor and celebrate my achievements, and acknowledge the wonderful work I had done to support my family and others. I was waiting to see me.

Then an incident awakened me to the fact that I no longer had to wait. I was laid off after fifteen years of service at a community health center because I had a higher level of education than my supervisor. I took that rejection as an opportunity to continue my process of transformation and complete my master's in social work, and I began to serve others while discovering myself at deeper levels. I learned how to be self-reliant, and built a network of women friends who became my extended family and ongoing support. And for the first time I did not feel alone.

I had to change the way I saw myself in order to allow others to see me as I am. I learned that in order to give to others, I needed to be able to give to myself. My mental clearing work, focusing on self-healing and self-sufficiency, led me to a Women's Healing Journey Retreat in Sahuarita, Arizona. We came together as women from all walks of life, sharing our wisdom. We were without watches, taking ourselves from limited time to unlimited and sacred time.

Being in a sweat lodge was part of our experience. I knew this was an important practice among aboriginal peoples, but I didn't know the how, when, or where it was done. I didn't know people of all ethnic groups could participate in a sweat lodge.

I discovered that the sweat lodge is a Native American ceremony for purification and prayer. The lodge was dome-shaped with a willow frame, covered with blankets and other available material on the outside to trap darkness inside. The lodge sat low to the ground, so we had to crawl into it like babies. I felt I was re-entering the womb. There was no room to stand. A round pit had been dug out in the center of the lodge. Large lava rocks that had been baked outside for hours were brought in and placed in the pit one by one. Like the four seasons and the four directions, there were four rounds of chanting, meditation, and prayer. At first I was terrified of this unknown experience. I wanted to run out during the first round, especially when the heat became intense. My heart was pounding louder and faster than the drums. I could not breathe. I sat by the door between two elders, grasping both their arms at the same time.

The sweat lodge leader sensed my fear through the darkness and gently comforted me. She told me to put my face close to Mother Earth and breathe into her to feel the coolness; to let go of my fear and the earth would take care of me. In that moment my fear was so intense that it didn't really allow me to believe that the earth would take care of me. Nevertheless I did as she suggested and was able to stay for all four rounds. I emerged from the ceremony with an inner strength I had never experienced before. One of the things I discovered through reflection on that event is that I am the creator of my own experience through the things that I say and do. I am able to see myself with greater clarity, with the ability to love and honor myself from the inside out.

The sweat lodge experience allowed me to notice a greater connection to spirit – and not only through my mind and feelings. I began to experience and feel things I had not done before. I'd always told myself that I didn't have night dreams. A good friend of mine told me that I did have dreams, but I didn't remember them when I woke up. A few days after I returned from Arizona and the sweat lodge, I dreamed that my son, who was then stationed in the Congo, West Africa, was being murdered. One of his arms was cut off at the elbow, and a very sharp instrument was used to separate his body into two halves. I woke up with my heart pumping a mile a minute. My first instinct was to call my son. Thankfully he was alive and well. The second thing I did was write down the dream as I remembered it. The next day was spent in a state of shock not knowing what to do with this information.

I consulted with my friend who informed me that the dream might have had very little to do with my son, but rather was about me and the shifts and breakthroughs occurring in my mind and body as a result of my healing journey. Viewed from that perspective, my son could be interpreted as being a guide in my life and in the very powerful and transformative process that was occurring moment by moment.

One of the practices I have continued since that journey is that of being still. When I am still, all outside influences and internal chatter are muted. In the stillness there is a knowing I hadn't felt before that journey. I trust it and give it access to a universal power to live through me.

As my journey continues, I let go of the remnants of the girl who once lived by compliance. I embrace the events that create and take charge of my life. Nowadays I decide where I go next. I am mending the broken pieces one at a time to see what I intend — wholeness and completeness. I declare my intention to embrace and expand my life with abundance, prosperity, and gratitude. It is thrilling to sit in what I call the "balcony of my life," looking out into the ocean of my world. I visualize my life as a space with a spectacular view as far as the eye can see. I can hear and feel a roaring energy like rough waves pulsing through my body. This roar is my own soulful being that I have chosen to reclaim. I no longer need permission to allow this roar to be heard. It drowns out negative self-talk; I am carefree. I have given myself permission to truly enjoy life. The sun is beaming brightly overhead and I am relaxed, comfortably settling in so I can savor all my discoveries.

As I continue to move through my life, my personal transformation is a mirror in which others can see the possibilities for themselves and take the first steps in the direction of their own changes.

Melissa Rowe, PCC, MSW, helps women claim their greatness and personal power, and take action in their lives. When she was abandoned by her mother at the age of sixteen, she had to raise her four siblings and take care of her abusive father. Melissa never knew the comfort and safety of home, but through her amazing journey she discovered home in her own heart and now helps other do the same. To learn more go to www.MelissaRowe.ca/blog.

⌐⌐

Let the Magic Begin:
Follow Your Resilient Heart™

Gail Saunders

"Five, four, three, two, one... BUNGEE!"

I DID A SWAN DIVE OFF THE TEN STORY BRIDGE where minutes before I couldn't get near the edge of the structure. My intention was to face my fears and take a leap of faith into the next chapter of my life. To my amazement, as I jumped into the abyss I felt no adrenaline rush, rather the opposite. I was amazingly held in profound peace. Back on the bridge after my jump I proclaimed, "If I can do this, I can do anything. I'm moving to Africa."

I had weathered deep grief for more than two years after my husband Frank died. At the time of his death, the capable, strong woman I knew as myself seemed to die along with him. I KNEW I needed to recommit to living wholeheartedly and not just going through the motions. I had slowly reclaimed so many aspects of myself that had been eclipsed by grief, so I decided consciously to fully engage with life again and to reconnect with my heart and listen for its direction. Heart whispers were encouraging me to reclaim my sense of adventure. I had felt strong pulls to Africa, tugs on my heartstrings. While visiting Namibia and South Africa with friends I felt at home there. I had listened and followed my heart's callings before, but this time was monumental: this time I was alone, freeing my hijacked spirit. It was a challenge not to let Frank's death be a stop sign in my life rather than a crossroad.

The ego can be very boisterous as it throws out doubts, limiting thoughts, and fears. I believe when I can hear and listen to my heart it keeps me true to myself and on my soul path. As I grappled with intense emotions and worrisome thoughts while mourning, it was difficult to hear my heart's guidance. Surrendering into a deep, relaxed state during a massage and energy session, I heard words from my chest, not my head. I knew this was my highest self calling me to wake up, get back in the game of life, and live with soul again. After the session my masseur said he felt I had a conflict about being alive and it was like a slow, unconscious suicide. The words from my heart were "I want to live!"

I made more efforts to meditate, get still, and bring my attention to my heart in order to be aware of my inner wisdom. Messages come from my heart in different ways. They might appear in the form of whisperings, intuition, repeated signs showing up, a dream, or waking in the night with a message. At times the communication is as subtle as a gentle nudge, while at others I am aware of a recurring thought with a strong feeling or chill bumps, "God bumps" as I call them. When I experience such confirmation, I know I am in alignment with my spirit and on the trail to a life of meaning and purpose, and I pay attention.

"Once you make a decision, the universe conspires to make it happen."
~ Ralph Waldo Emerson

When I made that proclamation on the bridge to go to Africa, I got out of my way and into the flow of life. The universe did step in and doors and windows began to open. Someone asked me to live with them for two months before I left California which allowed me to save more than $4,000. I arranged to go to a wonderful lodge in Namibia to work and live for three months. While there the owners prompted me to apply for a work permit and offer massage, energy work, and my artwork to the guests. This would also allow them the freedom to take holidays and leave me and another woman to run the guest lodge. My three months grew to be six profound years filled with such adventures as flying safaris, camping, wild animal sightings, and an archeological dig in a cave named after me.

The night before flying for Africa I had a dream. I was going to a formal dance wearing a flowing emerald-green taffeta gown. I was barefoot and my hair kept falling free from a French twist. My mother asked where my date was and I responded, "I don't need one. I will dance and have a great time on my own." In the morning I knew to silence my fears – that I would be fine. I was footloose and fancy-free, following my heart. I was more than fine in Africa; I reclaimed my sense of adventure. There, in that expansive, wild, and raw environment with ancient echoes, I had my renaissance among the oldest dunes in the world. In the birthplace of mankind I found renewed life. Thank God I followed my heart!

A resilient and unstoppable aspect resides within the heart. It is always present and available when you turn within. A spark of the Divine dwells there; our connection to spirit. I have learned to rely on this inner Wise One no matter what my circumstances. It is my inner gyroscope and it guides me back on track toward ME and feeling totally alive.

Another time I acted on my inner guidance was in my thirties. Frank and I did an exercise where we pretended we were eighty-five looking back on our lives. We wrote down what we would regret not experiencing or being. We had three things in common: live a simpler life, get closer to nature, and live in a different culture. After much discussion and deliberation, we followed our bliss. We quit our careers and planned to move to a Greek island for a year. That decision fulfilled all three wishes. We broke from our programmed careers and lifestyle as our old life just didn't fit any longer. The Chinese sage Lao Tzu profoundly warned, "If you do not change direction, you may end up where you are heading." Frank followed in his father's footsteps to become a lawyer, which didn't really fit his gentle nature. I was passionate about the arts: writing, art, and dance, but was told that those paths weren't practical or viable. I was molded to get my degrees in education and communications, and became a management consult for large corporations like DuPont.

When we first announced our plans to family and friends, not all of them were cheering us on. At first my dad thought we had lost our marbles. He couldn't understand how we could throw away our American Dream life and careers. We were determined not to let anyone sway us from our decision. We were the directors of our lives, no one else. He finally got on board and both families and friends said they were proud that we were following our hearts and making our dream a reality.

We were thirty-seven and it was time to forge the life we wanted, not one that was expected of us by others. Our motto became "Life is not a spectator sport!" as we formulated a plan to live life more fully and our way. Immediately the magic began. We received unexpected severance pay which helped fund our trip. More important, we were free to move in with Frank's dad and care for him when suddenly he was given less than a year to live.

After his father's death, we went to Greece via backpacking around the world for a year. This was the perfect antidote to the exhaustion of grief, caretaking, and settling an estate. Traveling quenched our spirits and our minds expanded as we experienced such diverse cultures. Finally we settled on the Greek island of Paros for our one year, which transformed into ten.

The simpler, more laid-back way of life captivated us. Our souls were touched by the sugar-cube homes cascading down the hillsides to the deep cobalt-blue seas and the fields of brilliant red poppies dancing in the wind to the sound of tinkling goat bells. The pulse of life was strong and direct for us there.

A few years after we returned to the states, my Frank was diagnosed with cancer and died at fifty-one. He was fortunate to say he had lived a rich and full life with no regrets. Not many people can claim that at any age. Too often people take their unlived dreams to their graves with them. If we had waited to live our dream until retirement, our dream wouldn't have been lived.

Yes, there were tremendous doubts and fears before we made the commitment. Sometimes it is easier to live by default or habit than by design. But when we decided to go for it, we experienced such exhilaration and empowerment by creating the life we desired. Every day, "I love my life" flowed from our mouths and spirits.

Many say, "I will follow my heart when I retire or when things are perfect." Things will never be perfect, and if you wait until then you won't do much. It is important to stay connected to your inner wisdom when things aren't going so well.

Numerous things in life have the potential to imprison your spirit. The captor can be a divorce, a loss of your job, financial loss, a trauma, an illness, or a death. Your soul often wants you to dare, to leap and stretch, to live outside the box of programming and limitation. Heart wisdom, the sage of your soul, will guide you to a tailored life rich with fulfillment and joy. You might start by humming a few bars of your heart song as you begin to be guided by your inner wise one. Singing a single note leads you in the right direction and can possibly build to a powerful symphony of fulfillment.

For example, my father lost his job at forty-five and followed his heart to law school which he had always dreamed of doing. He gained a zest for life that we, our family, hadn't seen before.

Jeanne, a friend of mine, once free from the responsibilities of caring for her mother-in-law, opted to go to Paris for a semester to study art. She was jubilant about her experience and felt like dancing on the moon. She describes it as her rebirth. For her, this was the beginning of a life of travel and adventure. Vic, a nurse I know, responded to her inner wisdom and went with Medicine Without Borders to Africa to help on a mission of service. This had been a vision she had held for many years and the fulfillment was more than she imagined. Lynn, another man I know, at seventy sold all his possessions and moved to Canada to study nutrition and alternative medicine at a university. He is living his dream with excitement as I type this story.

Another example is my friend Kathy who recently listened to her inner guidance and got a divorce. Although fraught with fear, she made the decision and then everything fell into place. She describes it as joyously dancing on the ceiling. Now she knows who she is and her personal uplifting song is *I Can See Clearly Now*.

Notice that joy shows up in all the examples of following your inner guidance. There is a sense of knowing this was the right thing to do. You experience an interesting blend of peace and exhilaration that comes from breaking through the barrier of limiting thoughts and fears. Orchestrating your life is truly amazing and very empowering.

Have you shelved your curiosity to explore new horizons and desires? Are you settling for a life that doesn't feel right? You don't want to end your life without truly living your authentic life, without ever singing a single note of your heart song. Go ahead, take a risk, your life depends upon it. What would make your heart sing? Follow your resilient heart; sing your heart song.

I leave you with this challenge from one of Goethe's couplets: "Whatever you can do, or dream you can, begin it! Boldness has genius, magic, and power in it."

Let your magic begin!

Gail, a global resilience catalyst, helps you create your ideal life by breaking through limiting thoughts and beliefs no matter the circumstance. She inspires by example, saying yes to life even after her beloved husband died. Residing on a Greek island, her compassion, presence, joy, and wisdom permeate everything she does, and she impacts lives through her books, coaching, workshops, and speaking engagements. Gail is the author of *Resilient Heart*™: *Transcending the Death of Your Loved One*. Discover your free Ideal Life Assessment at www.GailSaunders.com.

You Can Have It All!

Shalini Joshi Yamdagni

MY MIND HAD BECOME RESTLESS. My heart and soul had grown dry and arid, as if all the joy and inspiration I'd once felt had been sucked out of them by a huge vacuum. The faint, achy murmurs deep within my heart screamed out in pain, and yet I kept going about my life, ignoring the internal conflict deep within my soul. To squash these torturous feelings, I told myself, "That's just the way life is... you can't have it all!"

Aged thirty-eight, and married with two small kids, I still had no real clue about my life's purpose. After graduating with a bachelor's degree in psychology and a master's degree in social work, I found myself cluelessly drifting from one job to another depending on whatever showed up, whether or not it offered a better salary than the last job, and with no particular attention to whether or not I truly felt interested in and connected with the work I was doing.

In 2007, after being employed for five consecutive years as a training material developer, I started to feel frustration building up. Stuck at a computer for hours at a stretch without much human interaction, I felt spiritless, dull, and trapped at a job I had become good at. I desperately craved something different. Instead of a feeling of continued growth, joy, expansion, and satisfaction doing something meaningful with my life, I felt like I was gasping to breathe with each passing day.

Stuck in Victimhood

I found myself complaining all the time with colleagues at work, and at home with my family. My husband had recently started his own company, needed to travel back and forth, and was away from home a lot. I poured out all my frustrations on him and felt generally edgy and irritable in all my relationships.

The one thing that lifted my spirits during that time was watching a children's musical talent competition show on TV. But even that I watched with a sense of deep aching and a lot of jealousy. These kids were so young, and already had an idea of the direction they were headed in their lives. And there I was... thirty-eight and drifting aimlessly!

I recalled how, as a kid, music had been my favorite class. I was never an academically strong student. I worked hard to get decent grades. But music classes were like a breath of fresh air for me. I felt an ease and confidence stepping into those classes. Unfortunately there were no special voice-training classes at my school, just the regular music class attended by all the students. Wondering if music had been "my thing" and that the time to explore it as a vocation had passed me by made me feel even worse.

I spent a good deal of that phase of my life caught up in "if only" wonderings. "If only the boarding school had had voice-training classes." "If only I had not been in a boarding school, my parents could have found singing classes for me." "If only I could have a job I truly liked that also offered flex scheduling so I could be at home when my kids get back from school." "If only I had other qualifications so I could get a different job!" "If only..."

The Pain Speaks Out!

One morning at a gym, doing some abs exercises before heading to work, I noticed a slight, pin-prick type of pain in my left rib. A visit to the doctor got me a label for my discomfort: costochondritis – an inflammation of a ligament that connects the breast bone and the ribs – and I was prescribed a bunch of medications. But after months and months of going in and out of hospitals, the pain increased from a pin-prick sensation in my left rib to pain all over my upper body, with no sign of any relief.

I tried everything they (doctors, friends, family, well-wishers) suggested: a rib support, a neck belt, hot packs, cold packs, physiotherapy, ultrasound therapy, massages, changing pillows, changing my work chair, changing our mattress, but nothing eased my pain. Eventually I was advised to quit my job and be confined to bed rest indefinitely!

As a mother of two young kids (ages four and five at the time), I felt helpless, hopeless, and frustrated about not being able to be 100 percent present for them. One day as I was lying on my bed, my daughter, who was playing and doing summersaults on the bed, landed at an awkward angle and broke her elbow bone. As she cried in pain, trying to hold on to her broken elbow, I could only watch. Unable to get up and rush her to the hospital, a two-minute drive from my home, I found myself frantically calling extended family members for help. As my four-year-old sobbed in pain, I felt this piercing and heart-wrenching sadness about not being able to help, and wondered with absolute dread, "Am I going to be stuck like this forever?"

I grew up in a Protestant boarding school called All Saints' School in Nainital, a small town in the foothills of the Himalayas in North India. My parents lived in a remote town in Thailand then. Not having them nearby like other kids whose parents were in India, and not hearing their voices sometimes for a good nine months at a stretch, one of the things that brought comfort and made me feel safe was singing... singing hymns. I looked forward each school day to chapel time. It was my time with God, whom I viewed as my friend, my substitute parent, someone I turned to when things got rough at school. One of my favorite hymns was:

Ask, ask, ask and it shall be given you,
Seek, seek, seek and you shall find
Knock, knock, knock, the door will open unto you,
Your Heavenly Father is so kind...
He knows what is best for his children,
In body, soul and mind,
So... ask, ask, ask,
Knock, knock, knock,
Seek and you shall find!

Now, as I searched deep within my soul to make sense of why my life had begun to feel like a big, heavy burden, I turned to God. I was suddenly struck by the awareness that, in contrast to my daily chit-chats with God as a kid, I had somehow edged God out of my everyday adult life. As I had grown older, I guess I silently told God, "Thank you very much for all your support. I will take it from here!" And yet here I was, alone, disconnected, in pain, and begging God for help and mercy.

Sooner than later, help came in the form of a self-awareness seminar.

Awakening to the Truth

I still remember the email forwarded to me by a dear friend with the information about an upcoming "Self Awareness Seminar." My friend was planning to attend, and despite my obvious reluctance she managed to coerce me into going for it.

Still in massive pain, I popped a painkiller and tucked the rib belt under my shirt. Too embarrassed to wear the neck support, I massaged pain balm onto my neck and shoulders and headed for the seminar — the first night out for me in weeks!

As I sat there in the audience, I heard the host say, "We create our life with our thoughts. We create our sickness with our thoughts, too!"

Normally I'd have tossed that idea out as soon as I had heard it. But I'd just heard the host share how only a few years previously he had tried to commit suicide, had been cheated by his business partner, was going bankrupt, was going through a divorce, and was losing the rights to his kids. Now here he was going around different countries sharing his message.

The confidence with which he shared his message made me feel that he knew something I didn't. I felt a surge of excitement building within. I felt hope that there might still be something out there that I was unaware of that might help me.

Discovering Why I Breathe!

I signed on for a personal, one-on-one healing session with the host of the seminar. After the two-hour session, unburdening some heavy feelings from the past, I felt lighter and freer. My pain was very much still there, but I noted feeling happier and smiling to myself — something I hadn't done for a long time.

As I headed back home, I reflected on the session and my life. Considering the eight years of my childhood in the boarding school surrounded by friends, and my studies in psychology and social work, I realized I could never be happy stuck to a computer with no human interaction. I'd always felt good in past jobs that required working with people. But somehow all my negative feelings at work, at home, and in my relationships, coupled with a lack of self-confidence and self-trust, had weighed me down, constricted my vision of what was possible for me, and restricted me from exploring the possibility of finding work with people.

Now, feeling freer, my brain was scanning options for people-oriented jobs — public relations, social welfare organizations, human resources, sales. Out of the blue I had an experience that mere words simply cannot capture — a pure moment of extreme clarity when I *knew*! I knew what my path was, why I was alive, why I was breathing!

It's like every cell in my body suddenly knew all at once and without an ounce of doubt... that my path was "healing."

It was as if the heavens were pouring down love, joy, and light into my heart and energizing my soul, and I felt alert and alive like never before. I felt as though all my life I'd been breathing a restricted amount of air, and now it was a *full* 100 percent!

When I reached home I went straight to my bedroom, closed the door, put on music, and danced for a good two hours. I wanted to shout out and tell the world all about it, whether or not they understood my reasons for this joyful celebration. On September 9th, 2007, my life changed forever and I shed happy tears full of gratitude and joy.

From that day on the focus on pain was over for me. My absolute goal was to quickly heal my own pain and get on with my newly discovered purpose.

Healing the Pain

I signed up for a chakra diagnoses and balancing workshop with the same host. A whole new world was opening up for me... the world of ENERGY! Amazed and intrigued, I bought myself a library of books on chakras. But the host's suggestion about trying emotional freedom techniques (EFT) for my pain really got me going. I googled EFT, downloaded a free online manual, and discovered these strange techniques which I was told could help me with my physical pain. As I began to apply them to the best of my understanding, I noticed instant reductions in my pain levels. Super excited, I ordered all the DVDs in the online library and spent hours and hours each day learning, understanding, and applying these techniques by myself.

Interestingly, the focus of the techniques was clearing emotional clutter and old emotional conflicts about forgiveness and letting go. Yet after hours of *emotional* decluttering, I'd find significant reductions in my *physical* pain. After I progressed and learned more advanced ways to apply this method over the period of a month, I was free of every single pain in my body! I had healed my pain myself, and that was just the start! I now understood how our thoughts and emotions create our lives and "dis-ease" in our bodies. I realized that we are indeed the creators of everything in our lives, but that most of us are unaware of this and create subconsciously by default.

The Light Shines Through

Free from the physical pain, I continued using these tools for clearing out my daily stresses and remaining old conflicts, and clearing old, limiting beliefs as well. The more I cleared up, the more peace and clarity and joy I felt within.

Cleared and cleansed of old emotional dirt, scars, and debris, the light within began to glow, and I could feel it! A brand new me was born. I was saying YES to things I never dared before. I felt alive and energized, confident and happy, being me!

Eager and excited, I wanted to share this new gift with the world. But then my mind began its negative chatter, saying, "This is such a weird technique; nobody will try it. They will laugh, it looks so silly. Nobody is interested. Just be happy you're pain-free!"

But the overflowing excitement outweighed the fears, and I found myself asking a doctor who lived in my apartment building, whom I knew was suffering from leg pain, to try EFT with me. Amazed at the reductions in her pain levels, she began happily telling everyone about it. Word got out slowly but surely, and it has been an amazing six years now of my serving hundreds and hundreds of clients and expanding and growing in ways I never dreamed possible.

Living the Dream

Today I can truly say that I am living the life I always dreamed of. Truth is, it's far better than anything I could have imagined. My "work" and my life feel like a never-ending joyous journey of unlimited growth and potential. I seem to have time for everything I want to do: serving my ideal clients, family time, taking walks in nature, traveling to wonderful places, investing in self-growth, attending kids' school functions, and taking time to just be. As I move forward each day from a place of trust and surrender, I find that my days unfold with ease and grace, with lots of fun, magical experiences sprinkled in.

So I want to ask you, do you feel restless because you are sick and tired of being in pain? And have you tried different things but still feel stuck? Do you find yourself feeling edgy in your relationships, and feel a sense of disconnect with your life? I want to assure you that there is a way out if you are willing and open. I want to leave you with the three key discoveries that led me from my pain to peace and bliss!

- **Your pain is simply a message from your body** that something needs looking into. Something *inside* of you, not outside.

- **There is a direct relationship between pain and unresolved emotional conflicts.** Old emotional conflicts don't just fade away over time. They get stored in your cells, overload your system, and deplete your immunity, eventually creating pain and dis-ease.

- **Emotional freedom techniques** are simple, easy tools for deep-cleaning and cleansing these stored painful emotions.

As you clear the emotional cobwebs and your daily stresses, you will allow the light within to glow brighter and brighter. Your health, relationships, and life will begin to work *for you*, with ease and grace!

Shalini Joshi Yamdagni is a Physical and Emotional Pain Relief Expert. After doctors prescribed bed rest for the remainder of her life due to an illness, she went on a profound journey — and healed herself completely. Now she helps pain sufferers go from feeling stuck to relieved, and from frustration to peace and clarity. You can visit her website, www.EFTThailand.com, email Shalini@EFTThailand.com, or complete an online survey at www.EFTThailand.com/survey for a 45-minute free assessment session.

Become a Contributing Author in the Next Wave of

Pebbles in the Pond:

Transforming the World One Person at a Time

IF YOU WANT TO SHARE YOUR STORY in the next "Wave" in this series, and believe in the powerful impact one voice (*your story*) can have on truly making a difference, I want to hear from you!

Ask any one of the authors in this series and they'll tell you that it's been a life-changing experience to be a contributing author to *Pebbles in the Pond*. Beyond the accomplishment of getting published alongside some of today's most successful authors, you'll become part of a powerful "mastermind family," or as we've come to call it – a MasterHeart.

You'll make valuable connections and life-long friendships with like-minded authors. And you'll receive eight months of guidance and coaching to help you write your chapter and get started as a Transformational Author.

You'll also work with a professional editor to polish your chapter (so don't fret if you feel your writing isn't "perfect" – nobody's is). You'll receive an additional six months of coaching in my award-winning Get Your Book Done® program to write your *own* book, plus free attendance at the famous Transformational Author Retreat (a three-day retreat with your fellow contributors). Of course, you'll also receive your own copies of the next *Pebbles in the Pond* book – the one you will be in!

If you're interested in applying to be a contributor in the next "Wave," please email Info@ChristineKloser.com right away to get more details.

I hope to have the opportunity to work with you and see your story in our next book!

Many blessings,

Christine Kloser
Spiritual Guide ~ Award-Winning Author
Transformational Book Coach
President, Transformation Books

Connect with Christine Kloser

Website
www.ChristineKloser.com

FREE Transformational Author Training
If you want help writing your *own* book, visit:
www.TransformationalAuthor.com or
www.GetYourBookDone.com

Social Media
www.Facebook.com/christinekloserfanpage
www.Facebook.com/transformationalauthors
www.twitter.com/christinekloser

Mail
Christine Kloser Companies LLC
211 Pauline Drive #513
York, PA 17402

Phone
(800) 930-3713

Email
Info@ChristineKloser.com

About Christine Kloser

Christine Kloser is a Spiritual Guide, Award-Winning Author, and Transformational Book Coach whose spot-on guidance transforms the lives of visionary entrepreneurs and authors around the world. Her passion is fueled by her own transformation in December of 2010 when, after much success as an entrepreneur, she found herself curled up in a ball on the floor sobbing because she had lost it all. When she let go of the last shred of stability and security in her life, she discovered her truth and the blessings began to flow.

From that place, she fearlessly (and faithfully) went on to create the most abundant, impactful, and joyous success of her life in a matter of a few short months as a pioneering leader of the Transformational Author movement. Christine knows how to flip the switch from "broke" to "blessed" and shares her wisdom through her books, award-winning email newsletter, and speaking and coaching programs.

She's been featured in the *Los Angeles Times, Entrepreneur Magazine, Atlanta Constitution-Journal, Leadership Excellence, FOX News,* Forbes.com, *Huffington Post,* and Entrepreneur.com, and is a regular columnist for the award-winning *PUBLISHED* Magazine. Her books and publications have received numerous awards including the Nautilus Book Silver Award, Pinnacle Book Award, National Best Books Award, and Apex Award for Publication Excellence.

Her greatest reward, however, is witnessing her clients as they step into their true power, tell their authentic story, become published authors… and make their difference in the world.

After living in Los Angeles, California, for fourteen years, Christine now resides in York, Pennsylvania, with her husband, David, and daughter, Janet, where they enjoy a slower-paced, more relaxed lifestyle.

Learn more about Christine at www.ChristineKloser.com.